OPEN SECRETS
AN IRISH PERSPECTIVE ON
TRAFFICKING AND WITCHCRAFT

Dr. Jennifer DeWan and David Lohan

Edited by
Angelo Lafferty SMA and Gerard Forde

cois tine

Published by Cois Tine
SMA Justice Office, African Missions, Wilton, Cork, Ireland
www.coistine.ie

© 2012 Cois Tine

A catalogue record of this book is available from the British Library.

ISBN 978 0 9572521 0 3 (Paperback)
ISBN 978 0 9572521 1 1 (ePub)
ISBN 978 0 9572521 2 7 (Kindle)

CONTENTS

DEDICATION

This book is dedicated to immigrants who have made their way to Ireland and to all who have fallen victim to human trafficking.

ACKNOWLEDGEMENTS

There are a great many people to whom thanks are owed, without whose contributions this work would never have been possible and whose contributions enriched this work immeasurably. We wish to acknowledge all of those who contributed and to offer our sincerest thanks.

While this book is the result of a team effort which includes the combined talents of several people, Fr. Angelo Lafferty SMA, Director, Cois Tine and Mr. Gerard Forde, SMA Justice and Peace Office would like to extend a special word of thanks to Dr. Jennifer DeWan and Mr. David Lohan who voluntarily undertook the research and writing in response to an advertisement on the Cork Volunteer Centre's website. Their selflessness, talents, efforts, dedication and the enormous amount of time given are very much appreciated. Thanks also to the Society of African Missions Provincial Leadership for their encouragement and support of this work.

Dr. Jennifer DeWan would like to thank:
All the staff, volunteers and community at Cois Tine, who always made her feel so welcome, and who gave her such great insight and support for this research. And, of course, a massive thanks too to all who contributed to this project, with their knowledge and experiences of African witchcraft, who although they are not named were fundamental to this research.

Mr. David Lohan would like to thank:
Ms. Mary Crilly of the Sexual Violence Centre in Cork, Ireland and Sr. Monica Onwunali of The Congregation of Sisters of Our Lady of

Apostles (OLA) for sharing so many insights into human trafficking and prostitution. Thanks are owed too to Ms. Mary Murphy of the Sexual Violence Centre, Cork, Ireland for her assistance.

Mr. Phillip O'Connor, Director of the Dublin Employment Pact (DEP), for relating the work undertaken by the DEP, under an EU-funded initiative, to counter violence against women and the implications of this for anti-trafficking proposals presently before the Irish Government.

Fr. Shay Cullen SCC, Director of the PREDA Foundation, Inc., Philippines and a three times Nobel Peace Prize nominee, for conveying his experience of the realities of human trafficking in the Philippines.

Uachtarán Fhianna Fáil, Mr. Micheál Martin T.D., for the generosity of his advice and time in assisting the research of claims made in the *Trafficking in Persons Report*.

Mr. Alan Shatter T.D., Minister for Justice and Equality, and Mr. Damien Brennan, Private Secretary to the Minister, for their assistance in clarifying the contemporary position of the Swedish Model proposal, which would outlaw the purchase of sex, put before the Irish Government

His Excellency Michael Collins, Irish Ambassador to the United States, Ms. Norma Ces, Personal Assistant to the Ambassador, and Mr Martin McDonald, Counsellor for Justice Affairs at the Irish Embassy in Washington D.C., for their efforts in investigating claims made in the *Trafficking in Persons Report*.

His Excellency Martin O'Fainin, former Irish Ambassador to Australia, and the staff of the Consular Section at the Irish Embassy in Canberra for their efforts in investigating claims made in the *Trafficking in Persons Report*.

The personnel of the Office to Monitor and Combat Trafficking in Persons at the U.S. Department of State for their assistance: His Excellency Luis CdeBaca, Ambassador-at-Large to Monitor and Combat Trafficking in Persons; Ms. Jennifer Donnelly, Reports Office; Ms. Ann Karl, Reports Office; and Ms. Mai Shiozaki, Press Officer.

Dr. Marc Ostfield, Director – Policy and Global Issues at the Bureau of European and Eurasian Affairs at the U.S. Department of State.

The staff of U.S. Embassy in Dublin for their work in convening, co-ordinating and supporting the efforts of so many groups and whose support was invaluable to the production of this publication: Ms. Lynne Gadkowski, Mr. Peter Glennon, Mr. Christopher Rendo and Mr. Michael Hanley.

Ms. Marion Walsh, Executive Director, Anti-Human Trafficking Unit (AHTU), Department of Justice and Equality, for giving of her time to be interviewed and for her contributions in the form of preliminary data for 2011, the experience of the AHTU of witchcraft and the role of the AHTU in combating the problem nationally.

Mr. Barra O'Duill, Research Officer, Anti-Human Trafficking Unit (AHTU), Department of Justice and Equality, who facilitated the research behind this publication and through his expertise has directed the author to information subsequently deemed vital to the work.

Sr. Mary Anne O'Brien, Long Beach, Mississippi, for assisting with enquiries.

Ms. Fiona David, Research Expert, Trafficking in Persons Consultant to the Australian Institute of Criminology (AIC), for her assistance regarding the *Trafficking in Persons Report* claims of exploitation of Irish workers in Australia.

Detective Inspector Kajsa Wahlberg, Swedish National Rapporteur on Trafficking in Human Beings, for addressing the issues raised in relation to trafficking in Sweden.

Fr. Kevin Kiernan OFM Cap. and Dr. Attracta Lafferty for their support throughout.

Fr. Jarlath Walsh SMA for proof-reading the text.

Mr. Jerome Reilly, Deputy News Editor, *Sunday Independent*, Mr. Kevin Donovan, Cois Tine and Mr. Paul Donohue, Anti-Slavery International, for their contributions in making research materials on human trafficking available.

The staff and lecturers of University College Cork, College of Business and Law, headed by Professor Irene Lynch Fannon, and the College of Arts, Celtic Studies and Social Sciences, headed by Professor Caroline Fennell. Their many insights proved invaluable in dealing with the varied nature of this challenging subject.

PREFACE

This book has grown out of Cois Tine's pastoral care of African immigrants in Ireland over the past 10 years. Cois Tine (meaning 'by the fireside' in Irish) is a project founded by the Society of African Missions. It is motivated by the Gospel call to welcome the Stranger and by the principles of Catholic Social Teaching, such as human dignity, equality and solidarity – values also enshrined in the *Universal Declaration of Human Rights*. Since its foundation in 2002, its role has evolved from providing basic support and initial welcome for the newly-arrived to the provision of social, psychological and spiritual supports to long-term resident immigrants. This support facilitates access to services, participation in society and active citizenship.

Over the years, Cois Tine has supported thousands of individuals in dealing with a wide range of issues. Among them, we have encountered two very different but linked issues: human trafficking and witchcraft. For various reasons, these issues are cloaked in secrecy and therefore have been difficult to understand or respond to. In our experience, among members of the Irish community, there is a tendency to deny their presence in Ireland. On the other hand, many immigrants accept their reality but tend not to speak about them openly for fear of retribution or ridicule.

In order to gain a better understanding and also to find ways of responding to these complex issues, we decided to do something about them. *Open Secrets* is the result.

INTRODUCTION

Human trafficking is a shocking violation of the fundamental rights and basic dignity of the human person. It causes unimaginable misery and suffering as many are dehumanised and forced to become commodities that are bought, sold, used and abused. It might not be an issue we think about as existing here in Ireland but rather as a problem in Africa or Asia or other parts of Europe. Sadly, it is a crime that affects the communities where we live as human beings are trafficked into our country from other continents. Within the confines of ordinary-seeming apartments, houses and hotels, this inhumane form of modern slavery is taking place. Immigrant women, in particular, are suffering the consequences of human trafficking, which leads to a litany of horrific abuses. Victims are trapped physically, psychologically, spiritually and emotionally by their traffickers. This exploitation is often compounded by deprivation, starvation, torture and, in some instances, where African women are concerned, enslavement by witchcraft.

In a statement on migration in 2006, entitled *Migrations: A Sign of the Times*, Pope Benedict XVI criticised the "trafficking of human beings – especially women – which flourishes where opportunities to improve their standard of living or even to survive are limited".[1] During a visit to Angola in March 2009, he further expressed his concern about the persistence of the belief in witchcraft among Africans as he spoke about "Africans living in fear of spirits, of malign and threatening powers".[2] For those of us living in the Western world, it is important to try to understand these fears and that, for many, magical or witchcraft powers are real. They can have effects that are positive or negative, ranging from the insignificant to the devastating and should not be attributed to superstition. In communities across Africa, according to Michael Katola, a lecturer in pastoral theology: "Witchcraft is a reality and not a superstition. Many communities know these powers exist".[3] *Open Secrets* takes this reality seriously and does not judge those who feel bound by it.

This work, while primarily about human trafficking, also looks at witchcraft and how both are linked in the trafficking process. *Open Secrets* is part of an on-going process aimed at supporting African immigrants as they face the social, economic, spiritual, and psychological burdens of migration and integration. By exploring African traditional beliefs and practices (including magic, spirituality, witchcraft, sorcery, divination, oracles, etc.) and how they are manifesting in Ireland, we can better understand and ease some of the social, physical and mental burdens being experienced by African immigrants living here.

Dr. Jennifer DeWan begins with an exploration of the term 'witchcraft'. She goes on to examine its perception and understanding among Europeans and among Africans, where for many, the material and invisible worlds are linked seamlessly. In some cases, this link provides a means to control those who are trafficked. Further, by highlighting how African traditional beliefs and practices have combined syncretically with Christian beliefs (such as the Pentecostal and Catholic Charismatic movements), the foundations are laid for the development of pastoral practice and an understanding that does not necessarily judge or demonise traditional beliefs, unless the practices emanating from those beliefs are seen to inflict harm. By putting African witchcraft beliefs and practices into context with the Irish and European histories of witchcraft and magic, Dr. DeWan hopes to provide a sense of common ground, or a type of translation, where something first perceived as 'foreign' or 'backward' becomes more familiar, less daunting and more seriously considered.

In **Part Two** of *Open Secrets*, David Lohan explores the complexity of human trafficking and the increasing interest in the phenomenon. One must acknowledge with regret the growing number of people being trafficked into our country. Despite this fact, human trafficking is still largely viewed as being something that happens far away. Indeed, it may be said that human trafficking is now an 'open secret' in Irish society. Yet human trafficking is a complex practice with many different aspects. Misunderstandings abound concerning the practice and nature of human trafficking. Lack of understanding often means that awareness of the phenomenon is limited at best. This book seeks to raise both understanding and awareness and in turn, we hope, contribute to a greater and more positive response to this heinous crime.

This work is very much aimed at the ordinary reader. No prior understanding of human trafficking is required. The approach adopted by Mr. Lohan is one of a discussion on the topic. He strives to enable the reader to reach his or her own conclusions through his detailed research undertaken to present the case on human trafficking. Having discussed the tactics and strategy of human traffickers, he expands the discussion to include the world's only internationally-recognised definition of human trafficking and why it is important. The resulting understanding is used to develop a holistic comprehension of human trafficking, one which is mindful of tactics, strategy, motives, victim, trafficker and the consumer who ultimately benefits from the enslavement of others.

Highlighting some cases of human trafficking in Ireland, the text demonstrates just how very relevant the lessons of global experience are to Irish society. The origins and implications of human trafficking are explored, contending that the practice is rooted in human vulnerability. Human traffickers exploit this vulnerability to recruit a steady supply of slaves. Trafficking is a practice based on demand and supply. By exploring the supply in the source country, Mr. Lohan lays the foundation for an approach that questions 'who' ought to be criminalised and examines the links between prostitution and human trafficking in economic terms.

The contemporary situation of human trafficking in Ireland is explored through accounts of particular Irish cases. The measures already in place to counter human trafficking in Ireland, as well as those being considered by the Irish Government, are described. Mr. Lohan makes the case for a more sophisticated understanding of victimhood and cautions against reliance on simplistic stereotypical images of "hapless victims shackled to beds" and wants the reader to know the real impact of victimhood.

Victims of human trafficking suffer devastating physical and psychological harm. However, due to language barriers, lack of knowledge about available services and the frequency with which traffickers move victims, human trafficking victims and their perpetrators are difficult to catch.

Violence is at the heart of human trafficking. If one is to understand human trafficking, the role of violence in human trafficking must also be understood. It is only in this way that we can fully appreciate how so many can be exploited against their will, very often in public places and for long periods of time. Without this understanding, the true nature of human trafficking cannot be fathomed.

The Catholic Church condemns human trafficking. The Church's view is reflected in the words of Fr. Shay Cullen SCC, who has worked with victims in the Philippines for many years. He refers to trafficking as the "greatest the crime of all and it is one that has to be stopped, eradicated and the victims freed and compensated wherever possible. It is a task for the international community".[4]

The Catholic Church has a pastoral responsibility to defend and promote the human dignity of people who are exploited by this modern-day form of slavery. While Catholic Social Teaching does not provide a set of answers or a course of prescriptions, it does offer guidelines and directions to follow. In the **Conclusion**, the principles of Catholic Social Teaching are briefly described in the context of responding to trafficking and witchcraft.

This book is best considered as a source of stimulating ideas rather than one of definitive conclusions. It is written as an introduction to some of the challenging changes occurring in Irish society. It goads the reader into a realisation of the complexity of human trafficking and the need for greater awareness and understanding of the abuses suffered by victims. It also brings witchcraft into the open as a topic for serious consideration. Finally, it points to the need to formulate and mobilise a pastoral and societal response.

Angelo Lafferty SMA and Gerard Forde

---

[1]   Pope Benedict XVI, 2005.

[2]   Allen, 2009a.

[3]   *Ibid.*

[4]   This quotation was taken from an email sent to the authors by Fr. Shay Cullen SCC during the early stages of researching material for this book. The work of Fr Cullen is for many an inspiration and an example of practical pastoral commitment to the care of trafficking victims.

PART ONE

WITCHCRAFT AND MAGIC: AFRICAN TRADITIONAL BELIEFS AND PRACTICES IN THE IRISH CONTEXT

Witchcraft is a reality and not a superstition.
Many communities know these powers exist.
Michael Katola, Theologian

CHAPTER 1
WITCHCRAFT IN CONTEXT

*I must warn the reader we are trying to analyse behaviour
rather than belief.*[1]

This chapter begins with a discussion of the term 'witchcraft' and
how it is used, both in popular culture and in academic research.
The research process itself is then addressed. It concludes with a
discussion of the history of witchcraft and contemporary witchcraft
practices in Europe. **Chapter Two** moves to Africa, and looks at
witchcraft in the context of traditional religious beliefs and practices
throughout sub-Saharan Africa, as well as early Western
representations of African witchcraft. I then explore how witchcraft
functions in the contemporary moment, and some of the more
violent practices that have emerged in recent decades, including
trafficking, witchcraft accusations and human sacrifice. **Chapter
Three** takes the discussion to Ireland and to African immigrant
experiences of witchcraft. The final chapter in this part of the book
examines some possible avenues of response and thoughts in the
provision of social, psychological and pastoral support for African
immigrants in Ireland.

A DISCUSSION OF THE TERM

Belief in witchcraft and magic exists – or has existed – in almost
every society throughout the world. The term witchcraft is,
according to Ralph Austen, an "abstraction";[2] that is, it is used in
many different ways and includes many different types of practices
and practitioners, but generally it is associated with the belief in the
use of supernatural or preternatural powers, or magic, to influence

people and objects in the physical world. The English word 'witch' derives from the Old English 'wicca', which was used to refer to actions intended to influence nature, through a power (magic) not available to all human beings. Many societies across the globe engage in practices associated with influencing the natural world. In social science literature, these have been called witchcraft, or corollaries of witchcraft, including shamanism and sorcery. In many sub-Saharan societies, especially in Central and Western Africa, but also Southern Africa, both witchcraft and sorcery are terms used to refer to various 'traditional' beliefs and practices.[3] Sorcery is often seen to be interchangeable with witchcraft; however, in the social science literature and among witchcraft practitioners in the West, sorcery has come to refer more to powers that can be learned *versus* powers that are seen to be inherent.[4] Shamanism, a general term encompassing a range of beliefs and practices relating to communication with the natural and/or spirit worlds for healing, guidance and knowledge, often is used in the context of North and South American native beliefs. Shamanism has been used also to describe aspects of Celtic, Indian, Asian, European and African traditional religions.[5]

Anthropologists working in Africa have long tried to draw connections between African witchcraft and the European history of witchcraft.[6] Colloquially, when Europeans use the term 'witchcraft', it connotes images of women flying on broomsticks, large pointy hats and big black cauldrons. But historically, Europe has a long tradition of belief in magic and sorcery, as well as a tradition of punishing people identified as 'witches' for their perceived association with the Devil. For many Europeans, witchcraft is associated with the remnants of primitive (or 'pagan') pre-Christian beliefs and superstitions. However, this is not really the case: witchcraft beliefs continue to exist in many parts of Europe, both indigenously and through the migration of people from all over the world.

Some might argue that the term 'witchcraft' is too general – or too loaded – to be useful in describing the vast array of practices and beliefs in both African and European traditions. For the purposes of this research, we will continue to refer to aspects of both European and African traditional beliefs and practices as 'witchcraft': a) because that is how they are referred to in both academic work, the media, and popular culture, and b) because we believe by drawing connections between European and African traditions, this will provide the means for a more productive dialogue around witchcraft.

THE RESEARCH

This research was conducted as a result of a request from Cois Tine, a spiritual, psychological and social support centre for the pastoral care of immigrants in Cork City. Cois Tine sought to gain more information and background about African witchcraft, and specifically how it may be manifesting among African immigrants living in Ireland. This request emerged from discussions with African immigrants, who had expressed concerns and fears around witchcraft happening in the African immigrant community. The idea was to better understand the background for such practices, and how they fit into people's lives, in order to develop appropriate responses to help and support people coming to Cois Tine. There was also interest in using the research as an opportunity to draw some parallels to the Irish experience, in the hope that this would create conditions for greater acceptance and integration.

The research is intended to provide a broad contextual overview of magic and witchcraft. This includes a discussion of the term, its European history and contemporary manifestations in the West, the African context both historically and in relation to modernity, and how it is talked about and experienced by African immigrants living in Ireland. The research conducted was based principally on textual and ethnographic analysis, including anthropological and other social scientific books and articles; historical, religious, and spirituality texts; online and print news media; other popular culture sources from online research; and conversations with, and anecdotal evidence from, immigrants and the wider Cork community.[7]

Obviously, several constraints have disallowed a more extensive study, most importantly the subject matter. Witchcraft is a difficult, problematic subject matter to get reliable data on as it is a term that can cause a wide array of reactions, ranging from fear to derision. Researching witchcraft, and most importantly getting people to open up about witchcraft practices and beliefs, has been extremely difficult. Even in many African contexts, it is generally treated as an 'open secret',[8] where everyone is very aware that it is happening, but rarely do people speak of it openly – at least to perceived outsiders. Promising and maintaining confidentiality and anonymity were essential in people's willingness to communicate with me. In many cases, even with those assurances, people commonly began the conversation with, "It's never happened to me personally, but I know people who say that they have experienced it" or, "I am a Christian, so I don't believe in these things, but I know people who do ...," or something else along those lines. That is, removing themselves from the story even as they relayed personal narratives. The narrative – with a few major exceptions – was almost always about someone else's experience of witchcraft, and very few people I spoke with were willing to admit openly that witchcraft was occurring in Ireland, although no one denied it either.

As word spread that Cois Tine was conducting research into witchcraft, fewer and fewer people were willing to talk about it happening in Ireland. I believe this meant that, even though we were trying to assure confidentiality and anonymity, people were concerned at the 'public-ness' of the research. That is, one-on-one, personal conversations about a secretive issue are entirely different than public research. For this reason, I have provided no specific details of the original conversations that occurred or even any of the circumstances of those conversations. In one sense, this is to entirely respect people's desire for confidentiality. In another sense, it is to persuade those who have felt that it may no longer be safe to communicate their concerns about witchcraft to know that we have learned during this research that we must develop strategies for gaining greater understanding and providing better support for those experiencing problems relating to witchcraft, while at the same time maintaining the highest levels of confidentiality and discretion. I discuss the need for, and development of, appropriate responses more extensively in **Chapter 3**.

Other obvious constraints on the research included my role as the researcher, as well as time and geography. In relation to my role, it is important to note that I am not African or of African descent, and this outsider position might have determined or even constrained how people responded to me in interviews and informal conversations. However, I am an immigrant in Ireland, which created some points of common experience to draw on, even though the experience of a white American immigrant in Ireland would be in some ways profoundly different to a black African asylum seeker. In relation to time and geography constraints, this was a project conducted over the course of a year in Cois Tine, in Cork, Ireland. No doubt more time, resources and ethnographic research conducted in wider contexts would yield a more in-depth study. However, as this chapter opens up many possible research questions, I foresee extensive future research emanating from this work.

WITCHCRAFT IN EUROPE

Although witchcraft can refer to both positive and negative (good and evil) practices, in both contemporary social science literature and popular culture, witchcraft – outside of contemporary neo-pagan practices which are discussed in more detail below – has come to be seen as an explanation for misfortune, so it is generally assumed that any influence or change resulting from the practice of witchcraft or magic is evil or harmful.[9] In Europe, this has come as a result of the influence of the Abrahamic faiths' (Christian, Jewish, and Islamic traditions) belief in the Devil and the condemnation of magical acts, including witchcraft, sorcery and divination, in the *Old* and *New Testaments* (for instance, *Leviticus* 19:31, *Exodus* 22:18, *Deuteronomy* 18:10-14; also *Acts* 8:9).[10] With the growth of Christianity in Europe, witchcraft became more closely associated with the Devil and magical acts previously thought to be linked to a relationship with nature came to be seen as performed in worship of, and with the assistance of, the Devil (diabolism). Over time, the link between the Devil and magic in Christianity overshadowed all other ideas concerning magic in Europe and fear of witchcraft took a central place in the religious and social imagination.[11]

Traditional Beliefs

Although not much is known about this area, belief in witchcraft and magic in Europe is believed to date back to pre-Christian pagan, non-Abrahamic (that is, other than Judaism, Christianity and Islam) religions, including Celtic and Druidic beliefs,[12] and possibly to have even continued well into the early modern era.[13] In European traditions, witches were not always seen as harmful. There was an important distinction made between witches, sorcerers or warlocks who practiced harmful or 'black' magic, and 'cunning folk' or 'white witches' who practiced positive, beneficial 'white' magic, such as healing and midwifery. All witches were associated with some form of relationship with the natural and spirit worlds, as mediators to these worlds. Even though white witches were seen to do good and to counter the negative black magic practiced by 'bad' witches, white witches still were viewed ambivalently because of their perceived power.

With the rise of Christianity in Europe, many beliefs and practices rooted in local pagan and folkloric traditions, especially medicinal practices, came to be associated with the Devil (diabolism), and any form of witchcraft (and the person who practiced it) came to be viewed as diabolical in nature. Stories were told of witches flying about at night, using familiars (such as cats), killing babies and small children, drinking blood, devouring human corpses and cavorting with the Devil. Most parts of pre-modern Europe had laws against the practice of witchcraft, some even dating back to Roman and Germanic codes.[14] However, it was in the late middle ages (14th century) when belief began to turn into panic and accusations of – and punishment for – presumed witchcraft started to become more extreme.

The Witch Hunts

Among the Christian (i.e. Catholic and Protestant) populations of Europe during the late medieval to early modern period (approximately 1450 to 1700), fears around witchcraft and diabolism turned into a 'moral panic', a collective belief that Christianity was in an apocalyptic battle with the Devil and his army of witches. Scholars have attributed this moral panic to a wide range of factors.[15] Suffice it to say for the purposes of this research, it was a period of profound social, cultural, political, economic and religious change in Europe and that these conditions were certainly a factor in the emergence of a moral panic around witchcraft.[16] Texts such as the infamous *Malleus Maleficarum* (*Hammer of the Witches*), written by the Catholic Inquisitor Heinrich Kramer in 1486, defined witchcraft as practices of harmful magic done with the aid of the Devil.[17] The book described a variety of witchcraft practices, or *maleficium*, most notably the idea of the *sabbat*, defined by Ralph Austen as "an orgiastic sacrificial ritual presided over by Satan".[18] The *Malleus Malleficarum* also explained how to identify witches as well as how to convict and punish them, spurring on this moral panic. Large-scale accusations and 'witch hunts' ensued, resulting in the imprisonment, torture, banishment, and execution of possibly tens to hundreds of thousands of people throughout many areas of Europe, but particularly France, Switzerland, Germany, and Scotland. This period is now commonly referred to as the 'Witch Hunts', the 'Witch Craze', or the 'Burning Times'.

In practice, people who were accused tended to be outcasts, of lower social status, often previously accused of other transgressions and seen as having difficult or nonconformist behaviour. The majority of the accused were women and many of those were elderly and/or poor. Some were known as midwives or healers and therefore probably considered by some (perhaps even themselves) to be 'white witches'. Indeed, arguments have been made that the witch hunts were part of a patriarchal claiming of the realm of healing for men.[19] Accusations of witchcraft often were combined with other charges of heresy, including support of heretical groups such as the Cathars and the Waldensians.

Although mass accusations and executions began to die down by the early 18th century (the last execution of a witch occurred in 1711 in Ireland, 1712 in England, 1722 in Scotland and 1786 in Switzerland), European Christians emigrating to North America brought their witchcraft beliefs with them. This resulted in some accusations and executions there, most notably in Salem, Massachusetts in the late 1600s. The rise of the Enlightenment, and its promotion of rationality and science, gradually brought about a decline in the belief in the supernatural to explain the unexplainable.[20] In 1735, Great Britain passed the *Witchcraft Act*, which was meant to eradicate the belief in witchcraft among the populace by criminalising the pretence of witchcraft and trying 'so-called' witches, fortune tellers and the like as tricksters or con artists.[21]

By the early 19th century, belief in witchcraft had lessened considerably and came to be associated more with uneducated, rural ('backwards' and 'irrational') ways of life. Witches became the stuff of fairy tales and Halloween stories, relegated to pre-modern folklore. However, the correlation between witchcraft and diabolism has remained strong in Western popular belief and, to this day, fears of witchcraft bring occasional moments of moral panic in relation to fears of witch covens, satanic cults and ritual or cultist abuse and violence.[22]

Witchcraft in Ireland

The 'Witch Craze' was more muted in Ireland than elsewhere in Europe for a variety of factors, with only four known deaths (as compared to an estimated 26,000 in Germany).[23] Although belief in the supernatural would have been quite prevalent throughout Ireland during this period, some distinction was made between the beliefs in fairy lore and healing, and the belief in witchcraft as diabolical. The former was associated with the Celtic, native Irish, and the latter with the Anglo-Norman and Protestant populations in the country.[24]

Although belief in witchcraft did not create a moral panic equivalent to the witch hunts throughout continental Europe and Great Britain, there were a few prominent witchcraft cases. These included Dame Alice Kyteler of Kilkenny, accused in 1324, who fled while her 'accomplice' Petronilla of Meath was burned at the stake, and Florence Newton, the Witch of Youghal, who was put on trial for witchcraft in 1661. The last witch trial in Ireland occurred in 1711, after a young woman named Mary Dunbar accused eight women of practising witchcraft against her in Islandmagee, Co. Antrim.[25]

Belief in magic and the supernatural, associated with the Celtic traditions, remained well beyond the last witch tried in Ireland. It continued into 'modern times' in the form of stories of *cailleachan* (hags or witches), fairy changelings (such as the famous burning of Bridget Cleary in 1898), belief in diviners and wise women, and the practice of *piseogs* (translated variously as charms, spells or superstitions).[26]

Contemporary Witchcraft in the West

Since the early 20th century, there has been a growing trend, linked to the rise of the New Age movement, in neo-pagan practices and beliefs that use the term 'witchcraft'. In this context, witchcraft – or 'the Craft' – is recognised as a religion in many countries throughout the world. It is commonly seen as a nature-based or 'neo-pagan' religion that emphasises respect for all living things. Neo-pagans associate their practices with ancient traditions such as Druidism, Celtic spirituality, Norse and Native American shamanism amongst others. Currently, it is estimated that approximately 5% of people across the world identify themselves as neo-pagans.[27]

Wicca is perhaps one of the most prominent and well-known groups that define their beliefs as a form of witchcraft. Gerald Gardner, author of several books on witchcraft, is seen to be the 'founder' of Wicca in the 1950s.[28] Current Wiccan practice is still very much based on the writings of Gardner, who in turn was influenced by the work of anthropologist Margaret Murray. Murray argued that there had been a long-standing underground nature-based religion in Europe and that it was the believers of this religion that were executed during the Witch Hunts.[29] Practitioners of Wicca therefore associate their beliefs and practices with European pre-Christian, pagan beliefs and folk traditions – for example, 'white magic', the 'white witch' and the 'cunning folk'. Because of their association with the white magic tradition, Wiccans have a strictly benevolent ethical code governing their practices. Other popular witchcraft and neo-pagan traditions include Thelema (believed to have originated in the writings of Aleister Crowley[30]), Stregheria, Feri and Alexandrian Wicca. The majority of neo-pagans, Wiccans included, do not practice 'black magic'. Indeed, most do not believe in the existence of the Devil and do not worship a diabolical figure.[31] Despite this, Wiccans and other neo-pagan practitioners of witchcraft experience significant discrimination for their beliefs, principally through misunderstanding, and because of the continued salience of diabolical associations and representations of witchcraft in Western popular culture.

Historically, Ireland has had a strong connection with the rise of neo-paganism, as it can be linked to the development of nationalist ideals related to Celtic spirituality, fairy legends and Gaelic 'magic' in the face of colonialist British and Protestant rationality. W.B.

Yeats and Maud Gonne were both members of the Order of the Golden Dawn (of which the infamous occultist Aleister Crowley was also a member), which was a magical secret society popular throughout the British Isles in the late 19th and early 20th centuries. This Order is seen to have had a profound impact on 20th century occultism and the spiritual development of neo-paganism, especially in relation to Wicca and Thelema.[32] Ireland now has a significant neo-pagan, and particularly Wiccan, population and there are currently many neo-pagan traditions, celebrations and festivals in Ireland (for instance, the *Féile Draíochta*).[33] The Aquarian Tabernacle Church, an international Wiccan church, has legal status in Ireland and dedicated clergy. In fact, Cobh, Co. Cork is home to the White Witch of the Isles, leader of over 3,500 Irish witches and wizards, a coven that dates itself back 900 years.[34]

DRAWING CONNECTIONS

The European idea that witchcraft is inherently harmful has had a profound impact on Western perceptions and representations of indigenous witchcraft, sorcery and magical practices engaged in by people around the world. One obvious reason for this is that social sciences originated in the West – as the Western observation of 'the Other'. The categories early social scientists used to describe indigenous and native religious practices (witchcraft, magic and sorcery) would have been viewed negatively as they would have been contextualised within Euro-centric and Christian conceptions of the world. For example, the famous sociologist Emile Durkheim relegated magic, witchcraft and sorcery to the arena he designated 'profane' (as opposed to religion, which he considered 'sacred').[35]

Further, the way that people in the West have viewed contemporary witchcraft practices, and the more widespread Western fascination with 'the occult', positions witchcraft as an extraordinary opposition to the ordinary, rational, science-based world we live in. This perceived opposition also has had a profound impact on Western representations of non-Western beliefs and practices. However, this opposition does not necessarily exist in non-Western thought or ways of perceiving the world. We must find ways to draw connections with African and other non-Western beliefs and practices without assuming that they operate in the same ways that magic and witchcraft beliefs have operated and continue to operate in the West.

---

[1] Evans-Pritchard, 1976, p. 146.

[2] Austen, 1993, p. 90.

[3] I put 'traditional' in quotation marks because although belief in the spiritual world predates African postcolonial modernity, religious beliefs and practices continue to function dynamically and should not be seen as 'pre-' or 'anti-modern' (static or unchanging). By identifying them as traditional in my research, I am merely trying to signify their relationship to pre-colonial beliefs, and to distinguish those beliefs from post-missionary Christian or Islamic beliefs, although in reality these would all be mixing syncretically to form contemporary religious beliefs and practices in Africa.

[4] This distinction is discussed in more detail in the section on *Early Studies of Witchcraft*.

[5] Ariadne, 2007; Theodoropoulos, 2000.

[6] Austen, 1993.

[7] No formal ethnographic interviews were performed during this research (no recording or transcribing).

[8] Parish, 2010.

[9] JRank Science and Philosophy, 2011

[10] Belief in sorcery and witchcraft are also common in Islam – for instance, in relation to *taweez* (pieces of paper with verses from the Koran written on them which are wrapped in cloth and leather and worn under clothing) and *showest* (pieces of paper with verses from the Koran put into water and drunk), fortune-telling, astrology and numerology (see Bahman, 2010). Correlations between witchcraft and diabolism also can be found in the Islamic world, in relation to djinn, supernatural beings sometimes understood as demons.

[11] JRank Science and Philosophy, 2011.

12   Frazer, 1996.

13   Ginzburg, 1983; Pócs, 1998.

14   Gibbons, 1998.

15   Goode and Ben-Yehuda, 1994.

16   Gibbons, 1998.

17   Summers, 1971.

18   Austen, 1993, p.98.

19   Ehrenreich and English, 1973.

20   Ralph Austen (1993) has argued that the rise of capitalism in Europe also played a significant role in the decline of witchcraft.

21   Chambers, 2007.

22   Lanning, 1992. For instance, a public stir was created when a practising medium in the UK was sentenced to jail for nine months in 1944, based on the 1735 law forbidding the pretence of witchcraft that was subsequently repealed by then Prime Minister Winston Churchill in 1951 (Carrell, 2007). Helen Duncan was a well-known medium who travelled throughout the UK performing séances. She was accused by the British Government of using her position as medium to work as a spy, as during séances she performed she revealed knowledge about the sinking of British warships that was not public (Carrell, 2007). The *Witchcraft Act* was replaced with the *Fraudulent Mediums Act*, which itself was repealed in 2008 and replaced by consumer protection regulations. Incidentally the *Witchcraft Act* remains on the statute books in Northern Ireland, although it has never been applied.

23   Gibbons, 1998.

24   Seymour, 1913.

25   RTÉ News (Ireland), 2011a.

26   Bourke, 1999.

27   Health Service Executive, 2009, pp. 209-212.

28   Gardner, 2004a; Gardner, 2004b

29   Murray, 1921.

30   Crowley, 1938.

31   This is an important point, as the common definition for pagan when referring to historic and pre-historic religions is simply to refer to those that are non-Abrahamic, which would make Satanism a pagan religion, according to some religious experts (although others would see Satanism as a distinct Abrahamic religion). However, neo-paganism is unique from paganism in that it is a positive term, encompassing

specific religions, including Wicca, that do not have any belief in the Devil, so Satanism is not a neo-pagan religion (Vera, 2005).

32   Jenkins, 2000.

33   O'Brien, 2005.

34   Allen, 2009b.

35   Durkheim, 1947. The terms themselves – sacred and profane – which have had such a profound impact on the study of religion, are clearly very much positioned within a Judaeo-Christian view of the world.

CHAPTER 2
WITCHCRAFT IN AFRICA

Now that I have shown some of the historical and contemporary evidence for witchcraft beliefs in Europe and the West, this chapter discusses African traditional religious and spiritual beliefs and practices, including witchcraft in the historical and modern contexts. I hope that, as a result of the previous discussion of witchcraft in Europe, the reader has an open mind for a discussion of African traditional religious beliefs and practices. Instead of casting judgement that African beliefs are 'crazy', 'backwards', 'non-Christian', or 'evil', we can see that many societies throughout the world – including our own – believe in things we cannot prove factually or rationally. We will not be able to fully understand, embrace or aid the integration of immigrants into Irish society without making these connections.

TRADITIONAL RELIGIOUS BELIEFS

Witchcraft has become a common term used to describe some aspects of the collective traditional religious practices and beliefs of many African societies. While there are regional variations, traditional African religions, and the belief in the spiritual world that is integral to them, have many common elements across much of sub-Saharan and Southern Africa despite the ethnic and tribal diversity throughout this vast continent. This section will provide an overview of some of those commonalities of beliefs and practices. Because this section is preliminary in scope, I will not have the opportunity to delve into regional or tribal particularities or even into many particular practices and beliefs in specific African societies.

The majority of African religions believe in a God, the Creator of the universe, who is the source and sustainer of life.[1] African religions divide the universe into two linked worlds: the invisible (the realm of God and spirits) and the visible (the realm of human beings). Furthermore, the majority of African traditional religions are nature- and ancestor-based. After death, many African religions suggest that a person's spirit lives on in the invisible world and the living relate to them, especially through family or kinship networks. The relationship between the living and the dead is managed in a variety of ways, depending on the beliefs of the particular society. Practices to recognise or honour the dead may include symbolic offerings or libations, or naming children after ancestors. Invoking the name of the dead also can be used in taking oaths or making contracts. In addition, elements of nature (such as the sun, animals, rain, mountains, lakes, caves) have spirits that are respected and sometimes considered sacred. The spirits of plants, animals and people can interact with each other and communicate with, or mediate between, ancestors and people who live in the visible world.[2] This is the spiritual link to the visible, or physical, world; the link between human beings and God.

Spirits can manifest in many ways: through illness, in dreams or visions, through depression, or even a feeling of discomfort, through failure, or through divination. These manifestations could be to give advice, to warn of impending danger, to punish for immoral or disrespectful behaviour, or simply to pass messages between the two worlds. Illnesses or depression without any apparent physical cause are seen as having a spiritual cause. The spirits also appear in dreams and people can become greatly disturbed trying to determine the reason for the intervention of spirits into their lives. In general, dreams are highly regarded in many African societies as dreams are said to play an important part in three main areas: communication with ancestors, in witchcraft and in healing.[3] The spirits of the ancestors often manifest in dreams to complain of some failure in the living's traditional duties or the breaking of a taboo. Many dreams are seen as a type of oracle, foretelling events, revealing hidden or unknown things, but some dreams are seen as more clear than others. If the message of the ancestral spirit is clear, the dreamer may feel compelled to obey any instructions received or correct their failures. If the message is complicated or unclear, then finding the cause of the illness or meaning of the dream becomes very important.

By communicating with and following the instructions of the spirits, many Africans believe that misfortune can be avoided or success guaranteed.[4] Encounters between spirits and humans can be potentially dangerous though, particularly if they are misinterpreted. While most spirits are believed to be neutral, it is easy for humans to make mistakes or act in a way that is taken to be hostile or disrespectful. A spirit disrespected due to fear and misunderstanding may cause harm. Establishing the correct relationship with the spirit world and fending off malevolent spirits requires the wisdom and advice available from mediators who have learned the ability to communicate with the numerous kinds of spiritual beings that exist.

One important aspect of the spiritual presence in the physical world is the existence of mystical power, or 'magic'. God is seen to be the creator of this power, and people have a limited access to it through the existence of the spiritual link to the physical world. Magic in the African traditional sense can be used for both positive and negative purposes. People use magical power in healing, divination, exorcism, prediction, and protecting people and property, as well as in the practice of witchcraft and sorcery. According to African religious philosopher John Mbiti:

The positive use of this mystical power is cherished and plays a major role in regulating ethical relations in the community and in supplying answers to questions about the causes of good luck and misfortunes. For fear of witchcraft and formal curse, people may refrain from stealing, speaking rudely, showing disrespect where respect is expected, committing taboos against incest or doing harm to people like women, children, the handicapped, the weak and strangers.[5]

In many ways, belief in spiritual power is an explanation for why things – especially bad things – happen. But magic is also used to bring good fortune, health, success, love and protection, so it is also used to explain when good things happen.

WITCHCRAFT IN CONTEXT

The most experienced practitioners of magic are witches (whose deeds are referred to as witchcraft), diviners or oracles, and traditional healers or doctors (sometimes also termed 'witch doctors' because they can identify and cure witchcraft). The belief in, and practice of, witchcraft specifically by witches is quite common and widespread, though regionally variant, throughout sub-Saharan and Southern Africa. Although the term is used often by social scientists, the media, and other commentators to refer to a whole range of spiritual beliefs and practices that use magic, 'witchcraft' commonly is seen by Africans to be very specifically the use or manipulation – by witches – of the mystical power of magic for negative or evil purposes, mainly to cause harm to others.[6]

Witchcraft is used to explain misfortune, such as terminal illness or loss of property, enacted by a witch on victims ranging from close neighbours, family members, to random individuals. Witches rarely resort to spells, rituals or potions; witchcraft is seen as a "dimension of the person".[7] Witchcraft often is seen to function through the medium of consumption – witches are seen to 'eat' the soul of their victims through the spiritual ingestion of bodily fluids or organs, particularly those associated with reproduction, and even sometimes corpses or body parts of children.[8] This consumption leads to slow, wasting diseases in the victim that, without treatment from a traditional healer or witch doctor and identification of the witch and cessation of their activities, usually will result in death. In some societies, witches inherit their power from an ancestor who gifted it to them, either in the form of food or contained in some object that was bestowed on the person when their elder kin was dying.

Witches act using their souls to travel by night while their bodies sleep. In their soul form, witches travel to meet with other witches in their area (covens) and travel to other people to inflict damage on other people's souls while they sleep. Witchcraft also can function through dreams. Bad dreams or nightmares are seen as an experience of witchcraft where the witch is attacking your soul while your body sleeps. Dreams also may reveal a witch, persuade a person they are a witch or possibly even act as a prognostication of future misfortune.[9]

Witches also can use their supernatural powers to act on individuals or to manipulate other individuals to act without their being aware, such as through possession or by creating 'zombies' (which is widespread in contemporary South Africa).[10] However, because witchcraft is inherent, witches do not always know they are acting against someone; they may not even be aware they are witches. Jealousy often is perceived as the main motivating force for witchcraft and women are seen to make up the majority of witches, though when men are witches they often are seen to be more powerful.[11]

Divination is the "practice of foreseeing future events or discovering hidden knowledge through supernatural means".[12] Diviners and oracles can predict a person's future, interpret dreams, identify witches and detect the spiritual cause of an illness. Dreams sometimes can reveal a cure for illness, either by identifying a witch working against you or other spiritual causes, such as breaking a taboo. Diviners help people interpret their dreams, acting as a medium between the spiritual world, the ancestors and the living.

Medicine women and men (often called traditional healers or sometimes witch doctors) are found in most sub-Saharan African societies and are highly appreciated and respected in their communities. After significant training in the diagnosis of illnesses, knowledge of herbs, roots, insects, and other medicines and healing rituals and invocations, traditional doctors treat illnesses that affect both people and nature. They use forms of divination such as drumming and/or dancing to put themselves into a trance-like state, where they can communicate with the invisible, spiritual world – for instance, to heal spiritual illnesses. They also make and use medicines and perform healing rituals. Ingredients for medicines and rituals can include herbs, plants, seeds and other 'natural' products; animal parts, bones and blood (animal sacrifice is quite common); as well as items related to the human beings involved in the medicine or rituals, such as bodily fluids like blood and urine, hair and nail clippings.

Diviners, oracles, witch doctors, and traditional healers are all seen to have magic, though their magic often is ingested through magical plants or medicines instead of inherent as it is with witches.[13] Also, their magic is used mostly for good – to battle the bad magic used by witches. There is some level of ambiguity in this, however. For instance, in some contexts, witch doctors are believed to 'play both sides', identifying witches and curing witchcraft but also having the ability to practice witchcraft. This phenomenon – seen to be relatively 'new' (see section on *Witchcraft and Modernity in Africa* below) – was described to me in conversations with African immigrants from several sub-Saharan countries, including Somalia and Rwanda.

It is important to note that the magic – such as that found in medicines – that all of these practitioners (except for witches) use must be bought like any other type of commodity and, unless an adequate amount is paid, there is a danger that the potency of the medicine or the divination might be lost.[14] The fact that money is involved exacerbates the ambiguity around 'good magic' in that what one person may desire and be willing or able to purchase for their own benefit may have negative consequences on another person. Another example of this heightened ambiguity is in the witch/witch doctor doubling mentioned above, for if a witch doctor is both practicing and curing magic, in essence they are creating their own business.

Although they sometimes perform rituals or provide 'medicines' that could be viewed at the very least as ambivalent in terms of their contents or impact (such as love potions, protection spells or ritual contracts), traditional healers are not viewed as sinister in that they are not seen to be using their spiritual skills to inflict harm (like witches). Traditional healers also tend to have great respect for the powers of 'Western' medicine, though they are careful to distinguish between illnesses that can be healed by 'Western' doctors and illnesses that require their own expertise.[15] Their healing is holistic, treating the physical disease or misfortune and also the removal and prevention of its mystical cause (for instance, witchcraft or broken taboos).

Before the advent of Christianity, 'evil' was not associated with one primary force such as the Devil but was manifest in the actions of human beings using magic derived from nature or other destructive forces coming from ancestral spirits. Protection from evil was derived from the same sources of magical power (including ancestors, nature, and the family) as evil itself. In order to treat illness or misfortune caused by witchcraft, one must fight back against the witch, either by mystical or social means – or both. Ashforth writes: "either the malevolent powers are combated by occult or spiritual means, or the individual responsible is identified, induced to retract their evil powers, and punished (or cleansed and redeemed [with the advent of Christianity])".[16] Witch doctors, traditional healers, and diviners use their own abilities to harness magical power to identify witches and combat their evil. This includes counteracting the spiritual forces of witchcraft through ritual actions such as healing rituals, prayers, consultations with diviners, prophets, priests, or healers, and ancestral feasts, as well as neutralising the human source of those forces – the witch.

Struggles against witches are both spiritual struggles against the powers of evil and social struggles against ordinary people in the community at the same time. Therefore, what is important to understand is that witchcraft can be seen as both the cause and result of societal cohesion but also of significant societal tensions throughout urban and rural Africa. These tensions can result in much fear and suspicion, which can lead to communal rejection or abandonment, accusations, quarrels, and sometimes even killing, among families and communities.[17]

WITCHCRAFT AND THE COLONIAL ENCOUNTER

Like social science, colonial attitudes have had a lasting impact on our views of witchcraft. This has resulted in the large-scale suppression of witchcraft and widespread misunderstanding of how witchcraft operates within the larger context of African religions, traditional beliefs and practices.

When Europeans first arrived in Africa, they discovered a variety of traditional practices and beliefs, including magic and witchcraft. By transporting African people for use as slaves, European slave traders were first responsible for transporting ideas about African witchcraft across the globe, where traditional African beliefs combined syncretically with indigenous and Western beliefs in areas throughout the Americas. Religions such as Voodoo, Santería, etc. were feared, ridiculed and brutally repressed by slave owners and traders in the Americas because they were associated with slave culture. Indeed, Voodoo was even seen to be 'responsible' for the slave uprising in Haiti.[18]

The main role the next era of Westerners in Africa – namely missionaries and colonial officials – played in relation to witchcraft was to deny its existence, to suppress it through legislation, to treat it as a form of insanity and to promote a 'civilising mission' in the belief that, through a combination of Christianity and rational governing, Africans would cease their primitive beliefs and practices.

When missionaries arrived in Africa, their reaction to witchcraft beliefs and practices was to treat them as 'primitive' and 'backwards'. This was based in the modern Western rational assumption that witchcraft and belief in the supernatural was not 'real'. For example, the Church Missionaries Society (CMS) in East Africa presented the fear of witchcraft, spirits and 'superstition' as a form of collective mental illness or weakness, employing it as an important symbol in the battle against heathenism. In doing so, the missionaries conformed, to an extent, with the tendency of psychiatrists, psychologists and colonial officials to pathologise 'normal' or traditional African behaviour.[19] In this sense, belief in witchcraft was equated with insanity and dealt with by colonial officials as such.[20]

Colonial governments throughout Africa enacted 'suppression' laws in the 19th century meant to counter witch-hunting and the violence emanating from witchcraft accusations (as opposed to suppressing the practice of witchcraft, which was not given credence). These laws typically outlawed divination, witch-hunting and making accusations. For instance, in colonial Rhodesia (now Zimbabwe), the British made imputations of witchcraft (accusations and punishment of witches) illegal with the *Witchcraft Suppression Act* of 1899. This legislation also functioned under the belief that, of course, witchcraft was not 'real', so the best way to deal with the practice of witchcraft was to legislatively control what were considered the 'real' results of the beliefs – the accusations and punishments of accused witches.

The beliefs and practices enacted by both missionaries and colonial governments had little real impact on witchcraft beliefs, though they had a profound impact on the practices surrounding witchcraft. In effect, they simply moved the social 'control' mechanism of witchcraft underground (see *Early Studies of Witchcraft* below). Because both colonial governing and Christian missionaries gave little credence to African beliefs, Africans responded to their colonial presence by keeping those aspects closed to colonial outsiders. This allowed African beliefs to continue, even as Africans converted to Christianity, creating distinctly African Christian traditions and even churches, which continue to incorporate beliefs such as witchcraft.[21] However, it simultaneously introduced witchcraft into the law, which created other, more public levels for witchcraft to operate at – for instance, as an anti-colonial force.[22] Ironically, the arrival of Christianity also provided new discursive terrain for understanding the nature of evil, through the concept of the Devil. This has since become an integral aspect of contemporary witchcraft beliefs, especially in the context of the rise of the Pentecostal, Evangelical and Charismatic Christian Churches, which is discussed in more detail below.

EARLY STUDIES OF WITCHCRAFT

Anthropologist Ralph Austen has noted that comparisons between African witchcraft and European witchcraft have long been a staple of Africanist anthropology.[23] He states that almost all of these comparisons focus on "beliefs about such practices and the means used to counter them rather than on the practices themselves," and further that "all assume that beliefs of this kind have important social consequences and reflect the manner in which the peoples concerned understand their broader historical experience".[24] Although drawing connections between African and European experiences of, and beliefs in, magic and witchcraft are integral to this research, for the purpose of creating possibilities for mutual understanding, I am wary of saying they are *similar*. Following E. Evans-Pritchard[25] and more recently, Bruce Kapferer,[26] I see the categories ('magic' and 'witchcraft') as operating profoundly differently for Africans and for Europeans. For Europeans, belief in 'the occult' is seen as a counter to a rational belief in science, but for Africans, there is no such perceived opposition.[27] In the African context, belief in magic and witchcraft is very natural and ordinary as opposed to its perception in the West as super-natural and extra-ordinary.

Early anthropological and sociological interpretations of witchcraft in Africa – for instance, the work of E. Evans-Pritchard – were functionalist in approach, identifying witchcraft as part of a holistic cosmology or religion, a way of seeing the world and explaining it; it 'functioned' as a means of giving people a sense of control over their lives.[28] As part of an open-ended dialectic involving magic, divination, oracles, and sacrifice, witchcraft (and the resolution of witchcraft practices through divination and sacrifice) was seen to function as a "system of values that regulates human conduct",[29] restoring social harmony and providing societal cohesion. Viewed from this perspective, witchcraft was grounded in intimate relations between closely linked people, often peers, kin and co-wives, within a bounded space (a village, for example). People outside this close network – for instance, the powerful and wealthy in a society or people living far away – therefore were rarely invoked in witchcraft claims.[30]

Evans-Pritchard observed that, for the Azande people of Central Africa, witchcraft was considered organic, hereditary, an inherent quality. *Mangu*, the witchcraft substance, could be found in the bodies of witches, and grew stronger as the body grew, though it could also be 'cool' and remain inoperative. According to Evans-Pritchard, witchcraft explained misfortune and provided the means to respond to misfortune and bring it to an end.[31] For instance, if someone was struck ill by a wasting disease (such as those caused by famine), and believed they were a victim of witchcraft, their family would consult an oracle, giving the oracle names of people who might have a grudge against the victim. The oracle then identified the witch who was causing the illness. The Azande believed that a witch acted when motivated by hatred, jealousy, envy or greed. Oracle consultations therefore revealed histories of personal relationships: who hated who, who was jealous of you. A messenger would approach the witch, ask them to desist and thus the victim hopefully would be released from the witchcraft. Among the Azande, you had the right to (politely) ask a witch to leave you in peace and a witch had to adhere to custom and recall his or her witchcraft when asked.[32]

So long as both the victim and the witch observed the prescribed forms of behaviour, this would close the issue without any long-term effects on social relations (no violent responses from the victim's family, no enmity between victim and witch). It was only when the victim died, or the witch was seen not to have desisted, that things might become sticky and the victim's family might demand vengeance, which could mean death for the accused witch.

Vengeance also was rigidly prescribed. A victim's family had to go again to an oracle to determine what course of vengeance was required. Magic was used to attain that vengeance, oracles deciding when the magic had executed the vengeance and then the magic was destroyed. Witchcraft among the Azande thus was closely linked to morality. Uncharitable impulses such as hatred, jealousy, envy and greed remaining unchecked would have brought serious consequences.[33] Since the Azande believed that a witch could bring sickness, death or other misfortune at any time, this system – of consulting oracles, identifying the witch, communicating with him or her and effecting vengeance if necessary – was a way for the Azande to enter into relations with the unknown (witchcraft) and to control their own destiny.[34]

Since Evans-Pritchard, the study of witchcraft and magic has become one of the main areas of anthropological analysis because these concepts relate directly to issues around human nature, relationships and interaction that are at the "heart of the definition of modern anthropology".[35] Although Evans-Pritchard's work on witchcraft is seen as ground-breaking, the anthropological study of magic and witchcraft has come a long way since its functionalist roots. Mary Douglas was another prominent anthropologist whose work on witchcraft and sorcery has had a profound impact on our understanding. For example, in her analysis of African religious practices, Douglas found that, instead of the functionalist explanation of witchcraft as cohesive, witchcraft beliefs and especially the accusations that resulted from such beliefs could have a disruptive effect on societies.[36] More recent studies of witchcraft in Africa have noted that witchcraft can function as a form of social power. For instance, Peter Geschiere noted in his study of the Maka of Cameroon that people in relatively marginal positions in society use witchcraft to influence people with more power or wealth to redistribute it, levelling some of the inequalities in the society.[37] Other recent studies have linked witchcraft to modernity, the economy and the 'magical' movement of capital in the age of globalisation.[38]

All in all, anthropologists understand witchcraft as a discourse, or what Ashforth has termed a 'paradigm', around which people can pose and answer questions about evil. The witchcraft paradigm thereby functions as "a series of inter-related conjectures, suppositions, and hypotheses clustering around a central question: Why are we suffering?".[39] But more importantly, the origin of suffering can be attributed to a person or persons, so not only can the 'Why?' be answered but also presumably the 'Who is responsible?'. Witchcraft is a way of understanding one's own – and others' – place in the world. Witchcraft has been used to explain unfortunate events and disruptive social relations (for example, hunger, illness, crop failure, accidents, fights, family break-ups), but whether that explanation creates unity or disunity has been up for debate for decades.

In the social science (mainly anthropological) literature on witchcraft practices around the world, it has been considered important to differentiate between practitioners whose power is innate and those who learned their knowledge and skills from existing practitioners (witchcraft *versus* sorcery). Based originally on distinctions made by Evans-Pritchard in his famous study of the Azande, anthropologists distinguish between *witchcraft*, which is the power of a person to affect others by occult or supernatural means without necessarily being aware of it, and *sorcery*, which may be learned, and involves incantations, rituals and/or various substances or objects in order to affect others.[40] In this distinction then, witches practice witchcraft while those countering or responding to witchcraft practice sorcery.

This distinction is mainly to do with agency and intentionality. That is, if magic is inherited, then the witch's actions may not always be intentional, whereas if magic has been learned, it is understood that actions undertaken by that kind of practitioner are always intentional. For instance, in many African societies studied by anthropologists in the early to mid-20th century, witchcraft, or the power to influence nature, was found in the body of witches and was inherited. Among the Azande, studied by Evans-Pritchard in the 1930s, this substance was called *mangu* and was inherited by children from their parent of the same gender (all the female daughters of a female witch would be witches, but the male sons would not be and *vice versa*).

Witchcraft is seen to operate internally to a group, albeit underground, whereas sorcery is more open-ended and overt and can operate either internally or externally. This also links to the issue of societal cohesion for, if witchcraft is practiced unintentionally, by a witch who has inherited the power, then that person may be unaware that they are inflicting harm. So if they are confronted and desist, then societal cohesion is maintained. A further aspect of this distinction relates to the issue of morality, where witches are seen to be entirely immoral but sorcery is seen as more ambivalent – it can be used for either good or bad purposes.[41] Some anthropologists more recently have argued that although the distinction is useful in theory, it is not 'watertight' in contemporary practice, as many Africans have come to believe all witches practice witchcraft intentionally – that is, they practice sorcery.[42]

THE GENDER OF WITCHCRAFT

As I mentioned above, the majority of perceived witches in African societies are women. Although men can be witches, they are seen to be more powerful, more 'official', or more able to control their magic. According to Ralph Austen, "it is the *public* positions held by the men in question that makes their witchcraft somehow more tolerable and even, in some cases, celebrated".[43] A number of anthropological studies have noted how gender functions in the context of witchcraft, where female witches are completely stigmatised and sometimes even banished, while male practitioners of witchcraft often are seen as both witches and legitimate figures of political and religious authority.[44] The experience of being banished and the existence of 'outcast' villages full of women accused of witchcraft was vividly portrayed in a recent *National Geographic* video on Ghanaian witches.[45]

Women generally are seen to be the main instigators of witchcraft and black magic or magic purchased from a witch doctor or healer used to hurt others. Jealousy is often a main reason why women use witchcraft and/or black magic – for instance, jealousy between neighbours, jealousy of a husband caught cheating, etc. This belief was borne out in many of my conversations with African immigrants, who generally saw men as involved in witchcraft primarily as practitioners or producers of magic – not witches. This is not just true in African religious practices and beliefs; for instance, note my earlier discussion of witchcraft in Europe and the witch hunts that primarily targeted women. Zuhra Bahman has discussed the prevalence of women using witchcraft and the issue of jealousy as it pertains to witchcraft among Muslim women in Afghanistan, although the context, the belief systems and the social control mechanisms tied to witchcraft practices would be quite different.[46]

WITCHCRAFT AND MODERNITY IN AFRICA

New situations demand new magic.[47]

Modern Africa is characterised by profound economic, social and political flux as a result of centuries of colonial and postcolonial oppression and exploitation. Poverty, violence, the AIDS epidemic, famines, ethnic cleansing, corruption, authoritarianism and economic instability are some of the main factors that affect many of the countries that make up the vast continent.

With the influx of Christianity and Islam and the importation of non-indigenous ideas and practices through the diverse processes of colonialism and modernisation, many predicted traditional beliefs would fade and be replaced by more 'modern ideas' – Christian and Islamic beliefs, rational, scientific beliefs, etc. This has not been the case. In fact, beliefs in magic, witchcraft and sorcery have remained and transformed into modern beliefs and practices, sometimes combining syncretically with Christianity and/or Islam and indeed other 'modern' ideologies like capitalism that correspond to people's contemporary experiences of the world.[48] That is, traditional beliefs and practices do not always or necessarily make up a separate religion but exist in dialogue with Christian and Islamic beliefs and practices. Or they have become the means of 'fighting back' against the seemingly unchecked progression of global capitalism. Indeed, in some areas across Africa, there have been growing calls to abandon 'Western religions' and to 'return' to traditional, spiritual religions.[49]

The continued salience of witchcraft in modern Africa is very much tied up in the African postcolonial – and therefore hybrid – experience of modernity and reflects as much the 'hanging on' of traditional practices as the very modern disenchantment with the contemporary moment.[50] As Jean and John Comaroff note:

> *Witchcraft does not imply an iteration of, or retreat into 'tradition'.*
> *On the contrary, it is often a mode of producing new forms of*

consciousness; of expressing discontent with modernity and dealing with its deformities.[51]

Many Africans would be aware that Westerners might consider their belief in magic witchcraft 'backwards' or 'primitive' and this was borne out in many conversations I had with African immigrants living in Ireland. It is quite normal and common for African people, even very devout Christian or Muslim Africans, to believe and engage in all sorts of spiritual and magical practices, including healing, rituals for health, wealth, love and luck, divination, mediumship/fortune telling, as well as witchcraft.[52] In some ways, the African immigrants I spoke with suggest that witchcraft in contemporary Africa appears to be everywhere – in popular culture, in the media, on TV, in shops, etc. However, in other ways, witchcraft is often kept secret and not discussed, both from a sense that the forces at work are 'unseen' and also from a desire for discretion. For example, publicising that you had received good fortune as a result of magic might provoke jealousy among your neighbours. Or stating that you were 'cured' of someone's sorcery could not only be potentially embarrassing but also dangerous as it could get back to the witch who had perpetrated it, allowing them to redouble their efforts to attack you.[53]

Although witchcraft remains a potent force in contemporary Africa, there are many ways in which modern witchcraft practices and beliefs are profoundly different from earlier beliefs and practices, such as those documented above. In many ways, witchcraft has exceeded the boundaries of its earlier intimate social context and now functions in the global economy in much more profound and multiple ways.

So what is witchcraft in modern Africa? In his analysis of contemporary witchcraft practices in Zimbabwe, David Simmons quotes Gordon Chavunduka, President of the Zimbabwe National Traditional Healers Association:

Witchcraft in Africa includes the use of harmful medicines, charms, magic and any other means or devices in causing any illness, misfortune or death in any person or animal or in causing any injury to any person or animal or property.[54]

Geschiere has noted that contemporary witchcraft is now used to explain the misfortunes of modern African life, including inequality, injustice and conflict and most especially vast differences in wealth and prosperity.[55] One African immigrant I spoke with brought up car accidents as a common manifestation of witchcraft. He used car accidents as an ideal model for understanding how Africans perceive the workings of witchcraft. He described it as a 'common belief' that, if someone dies in a car accident, it is the crash that killed them but it is witchcraft that caused the accident. Success in any form – at the expense of someone else's misfortune – thus has become a result of witchcraft. People who move to the city and make money are seen to be successful as a result of witchcraft. Government officials who seem to succeed without popular support or to gain excessive wealth are seen to use witchcraft as well, or at the very least they are seen to be protected by and/or harbouring witches who act on their behalf.[56] Another person I spoke with discussed how football teams and their supporters used witchcraft to win matches.

Witchcraft has become tied up in the African understanding of global capitalism – a way of explaining how the few get so dramatically rich while the many remain so devastatingly poor. Witchcraft has become like the ultimate 'get-rich-quick' scheme, mingling with the rise in all sorts of other perceived paths to 'easy money' such as pyramid schemes and even prostitution (or 'small scale industry' in Nigerian slang).[57] It also has become tied up in the actual market, in the sense that the very materials for the practice of magic and witchcraft are now part of the global market. For instance, a recent BBC article noted that a simple ritual for good luck that involved slitting the throat of a goat cost approximately €280 in Uganda.[58] This is a massive sum of money for people experiencing profound poverty. Also, witchcraft and magic products are now bought and sold on a global scale for use anywhere African immigrants live around the world, including Ireland. Jean and John Comaroff have termed this blending of witchcraft and modernity as 'occult economies'.[59]

Criticisms of witchcraft, coming for instance from various Christian leaders or NGOs and aid agencies, would claim that magic and witchcraft practitioners, for instance oracles or witch doctors, are taking advantage of widespread 'ungodly beliefs' to fleece an unsuspecting and superstitious public by extracting high payments for magical services.[60] As I mentioned earlier, several people I spoke with talked about how witch doctors often also acted as witches, thereby creating their own business and ensuring their ability to profit from people's fears. While this 'system' of witchcraft beliefs can function differently to earlier beliefs and practices, such as those studied by early anthropologists, the objective remains, according to Geschiere, to maintain balance, redistribute wealth and level social inequalities.[61]

There are many aspects of the 'occult economies' of modern witchcraft that seem 'new', if only in the sense that the scale of witchcraft – the predominance of witchcraft practices in everyday life – seems to have grown exponentially. Whereas in the past, witchcraft was seen to function to a large extent within the social boundedness of kinship within local or village life, it now appears to have broken its social moorings and become 'globalised', transcending social and geographic boundaries. More and more, aspects of witchcraft are tied to more extreme violence and violent activities, including accusations, abductions, sacrifice, exorcism, trafficking and fatal illness. Some of these more violent or dangerous aspects will now be discussed in more detail.

WITCHCRAFT AND CHRISTIANITY

An important 'new' aspect of witchcraft in modern Africa has been its ties to the rise of evangelical churches, such as the Pentecostal, Evangelical and Charismatic Churches which have grown exponentially throughout sub-Saharan African. Makori has suggested that the rise and popularity of these churches comes from their emphasis on the personal experience of the Divine in everyday life and that this maps on much more closely to African traditional beliefs and practices than the more 'conventional' or 'mainline' Christian churches.[62]

Belief in the evil behind witchcraft has now blended with Christian belief in the Devil. Witchcraft has come to be seen as a form of demonic possession that must be battled through "spiritual warfare".[63] Pastors, or healer-prophets, now compete with traditional healers in providing healing to people believed to be victims of spiritual illnesses or demonic-inspired misfortunes. They also perform exorcisms or 'deliverance' to rid accused witches of their witchcraft. Pastors or prophets are given the power to heal and exorcise through their communion with the Holy Spirit and the relationship to the ancestral world this communion provides. Whereas prior to Christianity, possession was a common and often desired state of being, where one's soul could commune with particular spirits of gods in the spiritual world, with the influence of the Evangelical and Pentecostal Churches fears of demonic possession are much more common. These issues are discussed in more detail in the next chapter on *African Witchcraft in Ireland*.

Despite criticisms coming from Christian leaders in Africa and some Christian commentators that the majority of Africans are 'Sunday Christians' (they go to mass or services on Sundays but engage in magic and witchcraft practices during the week),[64] the combining of Christian beliefs with indigenous beliefs is neither overly complicated nor unique to the African context.[65] It also works both ways. The syncretic overlaps between African traditional religious beliefs and the influx of Christianity and Islam have had a profound impact on the interpretation of evil from all perspectives. According to Ashforth:

> *For the past century ... indigenous traditions of interpreting evil forces have been transformed under the influence of Christianity, particularly through the importation of the notion of demonic powers and the countervailing force of the Holy Spirit. Christian cosmologies have in turn been shaped by African traditions, and the largest and most dynamic religious movement of the twentieth century was that of the African Initiated Church, a movement directly engaged, where the so-called Mainline churches were not, in combating the destructive evils of sorcery, witchcraft, and demon possession.*[66]

WITCHCRAFT AND AIDS

Witchcraft has long been associated with inflicting harm through terminal or wasting illnesses and, in recent years, it has come to be associated particularly in the transmission of HIV/AIDS. Contracting HIV/AIDS often is seen as a result of witchcraft. However, the association of AIDS with witchcraft does not preclude people's perception of AIDS as a sexually transmitted infection (STI) or stop people from seeking out 'Western' medicine to treat the disease. For instance, psychologist Tamar Kaim found in her research on African immigrants in Paris:

> *Many HIV-positive Africans in France understand perfectly the way they physically contracted the virus as well as the biological course of their illness. And yet, simultaneously, they see a witchcraft attack as the underlying explanation for why they contracted the virus when and how they did. From this perspective, then, the antiretroviral drugs really do fight witchcraft, or at least the illness it causes (though strictly speaking they do not defend against further attacks).*[67]

Evans-Pritchard noted this phenomenon in his study of witchcraft among the Azande and I also noted this in conversations with African immigrants: the belief in witchcraft does not contradict with empirical knowledge of cause and effect.[68] For example, a man might have contracted HIV by having an affair with an infected person, but his jealous wife or vengeful mother-in-law would have set the mystical wheels in motion for him to become infected.

Witch doctors, or traditional healers, offer spiritual remedies for HIV/AIDS that can include the identification of the witch who has inflicted the illness on the victim. According to Ashforth, "while Western medicine pronounces that AIDS cannot be cured, thereby eliminating a potential 'natural' counter-explanation to the witchcraft hypothesis of 'man-made' illness, the course of the disease has its ups and downs, such that intervention by 'traditional healers' can very often seem, at least for a time, efficacious".[69] Some of these treatments can include physical and/or psychological abuse. And they also can be exorbitantly expensive, sometimes significantly more of a financial burden on the victim's family than Western medical treatment.[70]

According to Ashforth's analysis of witchcraft as a paradigm, the relationship between witchcraft and HIV/AIDS is not illogical. Witchcraft rituals often use blood, hair, nail clippings and other bodily excretions, so the idea of a disease transmitted through bodily fluids fits into a witchcraft framework. Also, HIV positive people can seem perfectly healthy but are described as 'sick' and the language used to describe the functioning of the virus can parallel language used to describe witchcraft or the actions of individual witches. He writes, "an epidemic such as HIV/AIDS that singles out particular victims within intimate social networks victims [as opposed to a plague or famine that is seen to infect all equally] can readily lend plausibility to the suspicion that malicious individuals are pursuing secret evil work".[71]

Belief in the relationship between witchcraft and the contraction of AIDS or other terminal illnesses means that fear, stigma and shame have become inextricably linked to the disease. This creates conditions that can tear families, neighbourhoods and villages apart, even as they are being decimated by the disease itself. Suspicion of sorcery, the fears surrounding witchcraft and witchcraft accusations and a general sense of spiritual malaise and insecurity produced as more and more people become infected and die as a result of the disease, brings profound uncertainty and societal tensions. As Ashforth notes, in South Africa, "suspicions of witchcraft ... cause recent quarrels within families and neighbourhoods to assume new significance, while old grudges and grievances will be resurrected and minutely re-examined in search of probable cause for the crime".[72] Many families keep it quiet that a family member is dying in order to stave off these tensions.

This also ties back in with the relationship between women and witchcraft, as women have higher rates of HIV infection than men – 61% of infected adults living in sub-Saharan Africa are women.[73] Women are more vulnerable on a variety of fronts in relation to HIV transmission – both because their subordinate status often makes it difficult to protect themselves against transmission and because women, perceived as the main practitioners of witchcraft, are often blamed for infection.[74]

WITCHCRAFT ACCUSATIONS

The rise of witchcraft accusations in recent years can be tied to the conflicting responses to modernisation and urbanisation in Africa. If witchcraft functions as a paradigm allowing people to answer the question 'Why?', it also gives the possibility of assigning blame by answering 'Who?'. This ability to assign blame allows for the possibility of both ending the misery and receiving justice. As Ashforth succinctly puts it, "knowing that *someone* is responsible for the misery increases the desire for justice."[75] Accusations of witchcraft are therefore an important part of the paradigm. Significant violence and bloodshed can result from the fears brought on by witchcraft accusations. Thousands of people throughout Africa have been tortured and/or killed as a result of being accused.[76]

While women and the elderly historically have been the primary target of witchcraft accusations, in recent years more and more children have become the main target of accusations.[77] 'Child-witchcraft' is now considered rampant throughout Africa and many children are abandoned, tortured, forced to 'confess' and sometimes even murdered as a result of being accused of being a witch. Although being accused of witchcraft often results in abandonment by parents or other family, children who are accused in many cases are already orphans or homeless and therefore particularly vulnerable. Widespread poverty, famine, war and violence, amongst other factors, has resulted in large numbers of homeless, unprotected children throughout sub-Saharan and Southern Africa.

Research conducted by Nigerian NGOs, Stepping Stones and the Child Rights and Rehabilitation Network (CRARN), has shown that belief in child witches can cut across "all facets of society",[78] from the poor and illiterate to the rich and powerful. People believe that children ingest a spell through food or drink, given to them by adult witches, that causes their soul to leave their body at night. The child is then 'initiated' into witchcraft and can use their power to cause illness, death, misfortune and destruction.[79] The Pentecostal and Evangelical Churches are seen to be very much linked to the rise in child accusations. Pastors have been known to keep accused children, starving, poisoning and torturing them to get confessions, to exorcise them, to stop the child's perceived witchcraft or to 'cure' them. The pastors also charge fees for exorcising or 'delivering' children.[80] Debbie Ariyo, Director of London-based Africans United Against Child Abuse (AFRUCA), states, "if a child is accused of being a witch, of being an evil person, and that accusation is endorsed by [a] Church, it gives people lee-way to perpetrate abuse on that child".[81]

Children accused of witchcraft often are stigmatised for life, caught in a vicious cycle, where even after exorcism or other tortuous rituals to 'heal' them,[82] they are never viewed as 'cured' and therefore always are suspect and at risk of future accusations. Where the exorcism or deliverance is not seen to have taken, or no one is willing to pay the sometimes exorbitant fees to deliver the child, children in some cases are abandoned or murdered. If they survive, they are extremely vulnerable, not only to recurrent witchcraft accusations but also to physical and sexual violence, sexual exploitation, exposure to sexually transmitted diseases and HIV, trafficking, abduction for child sacrifice and abuse of drugs and alcohol. According to Aleksandra Cimpric, in her UNICEF WCARO (West and Central Africa) Report, *Children Accused of Witchcraft*, "from a Western perspective, such practices are violations of the rights of children".[83]

The nature of witchcraft accusations – and the public forum in which they are enacted – makes it extremely difficult to refute an accusation even if one is in any position to do so. Because witchcraft is seen to be practiced in secret and relies on unseen forces, it is difficult to prove, but also difficult to disprove, if someone else is convinced they are the victim of witchcraft. Also traditional healers, prophets, ministers and diviners are all considered respected members of their communities, so when they have 'seen' and identified a witch, the community is inclined to believe them, for the sake of promoting social harmony.

HUMAN SACRIFICE

Violence in the name of witchcraft also includes the killing, maiming or dismembering of people for use in witchcraft rituals and medicines. Specific body parts or the body as a whole are seen to be extremely valuable in certain kinds of rituals, particularly those to gain power or wealth.

The sacrifice of a child is seen as one of the most powerful forms of ritual magic and has become an acute and widespread problem. For example, a recent study published by the Jubilee Campaign[84] and reported by the BBC, shows growing fears that many children are being abducted in Uganda to be used as sacrifices in rituals for wealth and good health.[85] According to BBC reporter Chris Rogers, the ritual was virtually unheard of three years ago in Uganda but is now rampant "seemingly alongside a boom in the country's economy".[86] People believe that the emerging elite are spending incredible amounts of money to pay witch doctors to abduct children in order to perform rituals that will enhance their wealth even more. Posters have been put up to warn families to keep a close eye on their children and campaigns have started to call for more legislation to protect children against abduction and child sacrifice. Although the Ugandan Anti-Human Sacrifice Police Task Force reports that there have only been 38 reported cases of ritual murder since 2006, the UK-based charity Jubilee Campaign claims that upwards of 900 cases have not been investigated due to limited resources.

In some parts of sub-Saharan and Southern Africa, albinos are often specifically targeted because their body parts are thought to have special powers. Albino body parts are used in potions to help make people lucky, healthy or rich. Albinos – particularly albino children – are being trafficked, even into Europe, for use in witchcraft.[87]

This chapter has explored witchcraft in the context of African traditional beliefs and practices. I examined how witchcraft has been represented by Westerners, including missionaries, colonial officials and anthropologists, and how perceptions of witchcraft have changed in relation to modernity. This chapter has shown that witchcraft can be both good and evil, an everyday phenomenon and the cause of extreme violence. The next chapter will explore African witchcraft in Ireland.

---

[1]   Mbiti, n.d.

[2]   Burnham, 2000.

[3]   Fisher, 1979, p. 220.

4   Burnham, 2000.

5   Mbiti, n.d.

6   This is an important point, which goes back to the discussion of the term in the **Chapter 1**. Although I acknowledge that many Africans use the term 'witchcraft' to apply very specifically to harmful practices, or indeed object to the use of the term at all seeing it as derogatory or misleading (Ashforth, 2001, p. 20), I use the term in this research from a social science perspective to refer to the broader range of supernatural beliefs and practices relating to sorcery, magical power, and the spiritual world.

7   Kapferer, 2003, p. 11.

8   Austen, 1993.

9   Fisher, 1979, p.222.

10 Comaroff and Comaroff, 1999.

11 Christoph *et al.*, 2000, p. 18.

12 Tlhagale, n.d.

13 In some cultures – for instance, South Africa – becoming a diviner is a form of spirit possession, where an ancestral spirit inhabits the diviner to help them communicate with the spirit world and give them knowledge of appropriate medicines, rituals and help effect healing. In the context of Christianity, good magic is seen to be imbued by the Holy Spirit (*ibid.*).

14 Evans-Pritchard, 1976, p. 97.

15 Ashforth, 2001.

16 *Ibid.*, p. 6.

17 Mbiti, n.d.

18 Thylefors, 2009.

19 Pringle, 2010.

20 Vaughan, 1983.

21 Tlhagale, n.d.

22 Geschiere, 1997.

23 Austen, 1993.

24 *Ibid.*,p. 90.

25 Evans-Pritchard, 1937.

26 Kapferer, 2003.

27 *Ibid.*

28 Evans-Pritchard, 1976.

29 *Ibid.*, p. 18.

30   Austen, 1993, p. 90.

31   Evans-Pritchard, 1976, p. 18.

32   *Ibid.*, p. 34.

33   *Ibid.*, p. 45.

34   *Ibid.*, p. 65.

35   Kapferer, 2003, p. 1.

36   Douglas, 2003.

37   Geschiere, 1997.

38   Austen, 1993; Comaroff and Comaroff, 1999. Making a link between
     global capitalism and magic and/or witchcraft is not unique to
     Africanist anthropology; see, for instance, the work of Michael Taussig
     in South America (1980, 1997).

39   Ashforth, 2001, p. 6.

40   Evans-Pritchard, 1976, p. 177; Hayes, 1995.

41   Kapferer, 2003. This distinction in morality would be quite different in
     the contemporary European witchcraft traditions, where for a variety
     of reasons, sorcery has come to be seen as malevolent in contrast to
     witchcraft which is seen as benign (Brennan, 2009).

42   Ashforth, 2001, p. 20; see also Kapferer, 2003.

43   Austen, 1993, p. 91.

44   *Ibid.*

45   Video available at: http://www.youtube.com/watch?v=woZCA12zdmc.
     Accessed: 16February 2012. See also African Women's Development
     Fund, 2011.

46   Bahman, 2010.

47   Evans-Pritchard, 1937, p. 513, quoted in Comaroff and Comaroff 1998,
     p. 279.

48   Syncretism – and, in fact, the global movement of witchcraft – is not a
     new phenomenon for African traditional religions. The mass
     exportation of Africans as slaves into North and South America and the
     Caribbean resulted in the formation of various syncretic religions
     and/or practices, including Voodoo, Obeah, Candomblé, Quimbanda
     and Santería.

49   Ellis & Ter Haar, 2004.

50   Parish, 2010.

51   Comaroff and Comaroff, 1999, p. 284.

52   This is not so different from fairly Western behaviours such as checking
     your horoscope, getting your palm read, etc.

53   Ashforth, 2001.

54   Quoted in Simmons, 2000.

55   Geschiere, 1997; see also Austen, 1993.

56   Ashforth, 2001; and Austen, 1993.

57   Comaroff and Comaroff, 1999; Nwolisa, n.d.

58   Rogers, 2011a.

59   Comaroff and Comaroff, 1999.

60   See, for instance, the Catholic Information Service Africa (CISA) website (http://cisanewsafrica.blogspot.com); also Foxcroft, 2009.

61   Geschiere, 1997.

62   Makori, 2008.

63   See, for instance, Moody & Moody (n.d.).

64   See Makori, 2008.

65   Though there is something to be said for Makori's argument that Christianity was embraced by Africans as an only every 'Sunday' phenomenon, whereas African spirituality is seen to be an all-embracing ('24/7') way of life (*ibid.*).

66   Ashforth, 2001, p. 21.

67   Kaim, 2008.

68   Evans-Pritchard, 1976, p. 25.

69   Ashforth, 2001, p. 10.

70   *Ibid.*, p. 11.

71   *Ibid.*, p. 8.

72   *Ibid.*, p. 11.

73   UNAIDS, 2009.

74   Ashforth, 2001, p. 3.

75   *Ibid.*, p. 12.

76   Cimpric, 2010.

77   *Ibid.*

78   Foxcroft, 2009.

79   Foxcroft, 2009.

80   Foxcroft, 2009.

81   Ariyo, 2005.

82   Gary Foxcroft of the Nigerian NGO Stepping Stones reports that, in the Akwa Ibom State in Nigeria, suspected child witches are commonly "abandoned by their parents/guardians, taken to the forest and slaughtered, bathed in acid, burned alive, poisoned to death with a

local poison berry, buried alive, drowned or imprisoned and tortured in churches in order to extract a 'confession'" (Foxcroft, 2009).

[83] Cimpric, 2010, p. 1.

[84] www.jubileecampaign.org.

[85] Rogers, 2011a.

[86] *Ibid.*

[87] BBC News (Africa), 2010.

CHAPTER 3
AFRICAN WITCHCRAFT IN IRELAND

AFRICANS IN IRELAND

Although it has not been well-documented, Africans have been emigrating to Ireland since as early as the 18th century, as soldiers in the British Army, freed slaves and abolitionists, domestic servants and economic migrants.[1] African immigration into Ireland after African decolonisation was relatively limited. The majority of Africans emigrating to Ireland before the 1990s came as students or spouses of European citizens. A new African Diaspora has emerged in the last decade, brought in part by Ireland's economic boom in the 1990s and early 2000s, a liberal social welfare system, good educational and training opportunities, transnational migrant networks and, until recently, a 'soft' immigration policy that allowed relatively easy migration into Ireland.

It also has come about as a result of a long history of connections between Ireland and Africa. Although Ireland never had a colonial presence in Africa, Irish missionaries did actively participate in the colonial 'civilising mission', which had a profound historical legacy in Africa.[2] In addition to missionaries, a large number of Irish economic migrants settled in sub-Saharan Africa during the 19th century.[3] In the 20th century, economic- and religious-induced migration turned to development-based migration and Ireland now has a significant development presence through both Christian and secular organisations such as Misean Cara, CHOICE, Concern, and Trocaire. According to Irish Aid, the Irish government's development assistance programme, approximately 80% of Irish overseas development aid goes to Africa.[4] The Irish presence in

Africa has left its mark in everything from street and hospital names, knowledge of the English language, the popularity of Guinness,[5] the study of Irish literature in African educational institutions and, of course, to the influx of Africans into Ireland.

As of 2009, Nigerians made up the majority of contemporary African immigration into Ireland.[6] Immigration into Ireland *via* the asylum-seeker method was a relatively unknown phenomenon until the late 1990s but, for various reasons, including the tightening of immigration restrictions elsewhere in Europe, it has become a more common avenue for Africans seeking to immigrate.

The recent African Diaspora has brought with it a rise in racist and xenophobic attitudes and behaviours amongst 'native' Irish. This has been exacerbated by the stereotyping and marginalisation of Africans living in Ireland, especially asylum seekers and refugees, disallowing significant levels of integration.[7] Racism has been further exacerbated by Irish government policy, including the fast-tracking of significantly curtailed immigration policies such as the *Citizenship Act, 2004*, which removed automatic citizenship based on birth in Ireland and the more recently proposed *Immigration and Residency Bill*.[8] All told, African immigrants living in Ireland can be characterised as a "peripheral people groping for admission into the hub of society",[9] and this produces profound instability and uneasiness.

AFRICAN WITCHCRAFT IN THE IRISH CONTEXT

There is growing evidence of concern among Africans regarding the occurrence of magic and witchcraft practices here in Ireland. As I discussed in **Chapter 1**, this research emanates from concerns raised about witchcraft by African immigrants coming to Cois Tine seeking social, psychological and spiritual support, guidance, even occasionally protection in the form of prayers and blessings, in relation to fears about witchcraft. Sometimes, it is presented as quite 'harmless', such as in relation to love or protection spells or magic to 'keep your man' or protect your children. Other times, it is seen in the context of harm, violence, illness or control. Anecdotal and documentary evidence of magic and witchcraft practices have been emerging throughout Ireland in recent years, including the growing popularity of witch doctors, witchcraft-related violence and the use of witchcraft to control trafficked people.

The majority of anecdotal reports relate to witchcraft and magic within the immigrant community in Ireland, particularly in the often stressful atmosphere of the accommodation centres. This is not surprising when considered in the context of the discussion of witchcraft in **Chapter 2**, where witchcraft is seen to be both the cause and effect of social cohesion as well as social conflict. Jealousy and competition produced by the stress of the asylum process potentially creates conditions ripe for witchcraft practices and accusations. For instance, one story was related to me of a 'suspected' witch in one of the hostels touching another woman on the shoulder and causing that woman to become so ill that her hair began to fall out. In some cases, witchcraft is thought to have been inflicted by disgruntled family members or jealous enemies in a person's home country – a testament to witchcraft's 'modern' ability to transcend boundaries. Another story related to me concerned a man living in an accommodation centre waiting for some word concerning his asylum claim, who believed he was under attack by witchcraft sent by family members in his native country for taking so long to get his residency and bring them over to Ireland.

Those who have expressed concerns about magic and witchcraft have done so in confidence, mainly because they are unsure of the response they will receive and also because they fear retaliation from whoever they believe is perpetrating the witchcraft on them for sharing their concerns with 'outsiders'. As I discussed in **Chapter 1**, when I spoke with people in Cork about witchcraft, their responses often were couched within the safety of displacement, where someone would be willing to discuss witchcraft happening in their home country or region, or willing to discuss witchcraft acting on people known to them, but rarely did anyone admit witchcraft had been enacted on themselves or speak in any detail about witchcraft practices occurring in Ireland. In addition, scholars of African witchcraft have noted that Africans often treat witchcraft as a secret because of fears of interpretation – if someone makes a claim that they are being affected by witchcraft, someone else many see this as a covert accusation or even an unwitting self-identification as a witch.[10]

In this sense, African witchcraft in Ireland operates as a kind of underground discourse that is also an 'open secret'[11] – that everyone is aware of but no one discusses openly. There are multiple reasons for this but principal to it in the Irish context is most likely the belief that it would not be treated in an accepting manner by the Irish population. In the time I have been conducting this research, I have presented aspects of it to mixed audiences of African migrants and Irish people and generally Irish people's response to the presentations has been a combination of shock, disbelief and humour. I believe this mainly stems from Western conceptions of witchcraft as something that belongs to the realms of superstition and not to reality; but it can also come from cultural misunderstanding and even racism and misogyny. This is nothing new and can be seen in Western reactions to African beliefs in the colonial encounter and in the context of slave religions in the Americas (see **Chapter 2**). Racism, misogyny and mis-understanding can cloud our understanding of the cultural, spiritual and historical context for witchcraft beliefs and practices, especially regarding the African witchcraft that is happening in Ireland.

Misunderstandings or disbelief surrounding African witchcraft in the European context also can be attributed to fears around what it may suggest – for instance, that rationality and science may not be the only explanations for how the world works. Political scientist Jodi Dean has suggested that witchcraft and other occult narratives disrupt the idea that there is a "knowable reality that can be mapped",[12] shaking the foundations of our belief in what is real.

This is linked also to what can almost be described as an obsession with (or fetish of) the occult in Western popular culture – for instance, stories of ghosts, vampires, communing with the dead that are so prevalent in Western popular culture. In the West, this obsession operates in a strange dialectic with the 'rational' disbelief about the occult. Just as African witchcraft has been linked to disenchantment with modernity, so too can the Western dialectic between obsession and dismissal of the occult be seen as such.

It also must be said, however, that, when coupled with an examination of Europe's and Ireland's own histories of magic and witchcraft and how many of these beliefs linger in various ways in the contemporary moment, I also have seen during and after these presentations an emerging acceptance of the similarities and connections between the European and African contexts and a growing awareness of the importance of intercultural under-standing in promoting integration.

AFRICAN IMMIGRANTS AND PENTECOSTAL CHURCHES

Pentecostalism is a rapidly growing religious movement worldwide, with an expanding presence in Ireland. Worldwide, Pentecostal and Charismatic Christians went from 6% of the world's Christian population to 27% in 1997 and this has been increasing exponentially in the last decade.[13] The Health Service Executive reports that, between 2002 and 2006, Pentecostalism in Ireland grew by 157%. However, this is seen as an underestimate because it is based on Census 2006 data and the major growth in Pentecostals is in immigrant communities that may or may not have been documented.[14] The majority of Pentecostal Churches cater to various African ethnic communities, though some of the congregations are mixed as Pentecostalism also can be found among the Polish, Roma, Filipino, Chinese and Brazilian communities in Ireland.[15]

The modern day Pentecostalist movement originated in the United States at the turn of the 20th century, but the majority of its growth in the last several decades is in Africa, South America, the Caribbean and South Korea. According to research conducted by sociologist Abel Ugba, African Pentecostal churches are among the most prominent social and cultural institutions established by new African immigrants living in Ireland. These churches are, Ugba claims, "facilitating communication and interaction among their members, providing physical, social and emotional help to the needy, and helping members understand and cope with their situation of voluntary or involuntary exile".[16]

Because of their rootedness in traditional beliefs and practices, African Pentecostals believe many illnesses and other misfortunes are caused by diabolical forces or witches. African Pentecostals rely on their pastor – as opposed to a witch doctor or traditional healer or diviner – to help them. The pastor uses prayer, rituals of anointing and singing, in order to heal based on power given through divine intervention. In some cases, pastors perform exorcisms, or 'deliverance' ceremonies, to force out demonic spirits from people.[17] The use of exorcism in Pentecostalism is not unique to Africa – indeed, exorcism or deliverance is quite commonplace among Pentecostals and Catholic Charismatics groups in North America.[18] In the African context, however, exorcism often is linked to witchcraft and those perceived to be possessed also are called witches. Exorcism rituals tied to witchcraft, particularly among children, have been on the rise in African countries but also reportedly in the UK.[19] In extreme cases, exorcism is no simple deliverance prayer but a violent experience replete with poison, burning, torture, drowning, beating, etc. Journalist Cindi John reported several cases of violent child exorcisms in the UK in recent years related to African Pentecostal churches.[20]

It is important to note that, as far as I am aware, no anecdotal evidence or reports have emerged that these violent forms of exorcism are occurring among African Pentecostals in Ireland. Presumably the more peaceful deliverance ceremonies, since they are such an integral part of many Pentecostal and Charismatic churches, are happening. This is certainly an area that requires additional research.

WITCHCRAFT AND TRAFFICKING

Magic and witchcraft reportedly are used in cases of human trafficking, where adults and children, most often women and girls, are illegally traded like commodities for use in sex work and sexual exploitation, forced labour, slavery, or organ removal. The second part of this book discusses human trafficking in the Irish context in more detail.

Magic and witchcraft most commonly are used as oaths to 'bind' trafficked or smuggled people to their traffickers, so that they will not try to escape, and to ensure that the trafficked person pays back to the trafficker the often exorbitant fee demanded for getting them to the contracted destination. In Nigeria, and particularly in the state of Edo, from where a large proportion of the women and girls trafficked into Europe originate, 'Juju' binding rituals are performed by traditional healers, using things like nail clippings or hair, to bind the woman to her trafficker, to ensure that she stays where she is sent and pays back her debt.[21] The Juju 'priest' or healer then holds onto the pieces from the woman's body, so that a part of her remains in Nigeria even after she has left and this will protect her as well as keep her bound to her oath. If she goes against her contract, bad things will happen to her and her family. In many cases, only the traditional healer who performed the original ritual can perform the additional ritual to break the contract. Although these oaths often are called 'witchcraft' by the international media, policy-makers and law enforcement, several Nigerian immigrants were careful to remind me that this is not 'witchcraft' in an African sense because the magic is not performed by a witch on an unsuspecting individual.

In its most recent *Annual Statistics Report*, Ruhama, an Irish organisation dedicated to supporting women affected by prostitution and sex trafficking, reported a number of cases where some form of witchcraft had been used to control trafficked women living in Ireland.[22] The first report of the Department of Justice's Anti-Human Trafficking Unit (AHTU) in 2010 corroborated this evidence. The report stated that AHTU was investigating 66 trafficking cases involving witchcraft but that the actual number could be much higher, "due to the clandestine nature of the crime and its overlap with other illegal activities".[23]

In 2010, a couple was jailed in Wales for running a prostitution ring that included approximately 35 brothels in the Republic of Ireland. They were using girls trafficked from Nigeria, some of whom had been terrified into working for fear of breaking the Juju oath they had made before leaving Nigeria. Although the couple was not involved directly in trafficking, the trafficked women, some as young as 15, reportedly suffered continual terrorising at the hands of their traffickers, which included having to sleep in a coffin, eating raw chicken hearts and having fingernail clippings and pubic hair collected and kept for use in witchcraft practices and charms (see **Part Two** of this book for more on this case). In addition, they were forced to promise to pay back the cost (£65,000) of their own trafficking.[24]

This is not uncommon throughout Europe and has been reported in places like Sweden and Italy, both anecdotally[25] and in the press.[26] Girls are being trafficked into Europe as sex workers, in many cases by their own families, to earn money to send back home. In many cases, witchcraft and magic are being used in various ways by the families, by the traffickers and by the women themselves.

For example, an article in *Newswatch*, a Nigerian weekly tabloid newspaper, stated in 1999 that Nigerian girls consult oracles before heading off to Italy to 'do work' to find out their fate: "If the oracle says a girl cannot make it in Italy, she petitions 'our ancestors' to reverse the bad fate ... to get 'the ancestors' to intercede on her behalf".[27] According to this article, pastors in Pentecostal churches often act as oracles as well, asking for girls to bring offerings, including chickens, eggs, goats, yams and palm oil, in order to perform sacrifices with the items to determine how successful the girl will be in her venture.[28] It further notes that witchcraft is used between trafficked women living in Europe, in fights over status, customers, money, etc. They write to their families to get a witch doctor to prepare magic spells for them – for instance, to make another woman smell bad ('like a goat') and turn off customers, which is then mailed to her by special postage or courier. Ofuoko reports that parents also send their daughters charms to attract customers, or to get customers to spend more money, as well as fetish objects, anointing oils and other witchcraft 'products'. There also have been reports of women using love potions to lure a European man into marrying them, so they can stay in Europe legally. In some cases, witch doctors are flown to Italy by the family to bring charms or cast spells in person.

In addition to the sex trade, traffickers also are bringing women and children into Europe for human sacrificial purposes. Many NGOs and aid agencies working in Africa have noted the correlations between child abandonment, child witchcraft accusations, child abduction and child trafficking.[29] For example, there was the case of the mutilated body of a boy found in the Thames in 2002. The limbs and head of the young boy had been amputated, purportedly to use in spells to cure ailments from impotence to bad sight.[30] In 2005, the beheaded body of a Malawi woman was found in Kilkenny. It is believed she was murdered and her head taken for ritual purposes, either for not returning to work in a brothel in Kilkenny, or because she had not fully paid back her traffickers. Her killers are believed to be Nigerian, but have never been found.[31]

---

[1]   Ejorh, n.d., p. 3; Ugba, 2004, p. 2.

[2]   Ejorh, n.d., p. 1.

3   *Ibid.*, p. 2.

4   Irish Aid, 2011.

5   Nigeria is Guinness' third largest market, while Ghana, Cameroon and
    Kenya are in the top 10 (Ejorh, n.d., p.2). About 40% of Guinness' total
    world production is brewed and sold in Africa
    (http://en.wikipedia.org/wiki/Guinness - cite_note-66).

6   Ugba, 2009.

7   Fanning *et al.*, 2011.

8   NGO Alliance Against Racism, 2011.

9   Ejorh, n.d., p. 4.

10 Parish, 2010.

11 *Ibid.*, p. 79.

12 Dean, 2002, p. 93.

13 Ugba, 2009, p. 49.

14 Health Service Executive, 2009.

15 Pentecostalism is practiced by approximately 70% of the Roma
    community living in Ireland (*ibid.*).

16 Ugba, 2009, p. 40.

17 In the spirit of cultural relativism, it is important to keep in mind that
    exorcisms are practiced – in varying forms – throughout the world,
    including the 'Christian West'. They are, in fact, on the rise in Roman
    Catholic and Orthodox Christian contexts (BBC News, 2005; Goodstein,
    2010).

18 Csordas, 1994.

19 John, 2005.

20 *Ibid.*

21 UNESCO, 2006.

22 Ruhama, 2011.

23 O'Doherty, 2010.

24 Davies, 2010.

25 Dorothy Zinn, personal communication.

26 Ofuoku, 1999; Polisen, 2010.

27 Ofuoku, 1999.

28 *Ibid.*

29 Cimpric, 2010; Foxcroft, 2009.

30 Harris, 2002.

31 Cusack, 2010a.

CHAPTER 4
TOWARDS UNDERSTANDING AND SUPPORT

Witchcraft is a notion so foreign to us that it is hard for us to appreciate ... convictions about its reality.[1]

Ireland is a considerably more diverse country now than it was even a few decades ago and part of embracing this diversity is building our awareness of the other cultural practices and beliefs that make up a part of Irish society today. African immigrants experience many obstacles to integrating into Irish society. In an age of rationality and reason, we may feel on the surface unprepared with how to relate to people who believe in witchcraft, magic, and the supernatural and how best to provide them with support and counsel. The issue here is not to determine whether these things actually exist but to acknowledge that these beliefs and practices are happening and to try and understand them better, without judging them automatically as 'irrational', 'illogical', 'backwards' or 'evil', or that integration will bring an 'inevitable' fading away of these beliefs. It is also to determine how best to handle practically the ways in which these beliefs manifest themselves, the fear and distress they may cause and the possible violence that may result.

CULTURAL

An integral part in helping people to deal with concerns about witchcraft is to be aware of our own biases and ethnocentrism, be tolerant and open-minded and embrace cultural relativism in relation to other people's cultural beliefs, practices and heritage.

Cultural relativism is based in the idea that people's beliefs and practices should be judged in the context of their own culture. It holds that there is nothing to be gained by judging other cultures against the values of our own. We will not be able to provide needed support if we are more concerned with convincing others that what they believe is not happening, is irrational, or evil.

In organisational contexts, cultural relativism is often defined as 'interculturalism', the "willingness and capacity of an organisation to ensure that cultural difference is acknowledged, respected and provided for in a planned and systematic way in all systems, processes and practices".[2] The Health Service Executive's *Intercultural Guide* states that an intercultural approach includes:

- Awareness of one's own cultural values.

- Awareness and understanding that people of different cultures have different beliefs, ways of communicating, interacting, behaving and responding.

- Appreciating that cultural and spiritual beliefs impact patients' health and health-related beliefs, help-seeking behaviour, interactions with health care professionals and health care practices.

- A willingness and capacity to respond appropriately to patients' cultural and/or ethnic background in order to provide optimal care for the patient.[3]

If necessary, cultural mediation can be helpful in organisational settings to help bridge cultural gaps between yourself and another person. Cultural mediation is "a dynamic process through which a professionally trained third party acts as a cultural broker between a person using a service and the service provider, to help them both to reach a common understanding which will ultimately lead to more satisfactory outcomes in service provision and use".[4]

Cultural relativism or interculturalism, of course, is distinct from moral relativism, where different cultural norms are deemed to have equal moral value. When there is violence involved, such as in the relation to trafficking, torture, or any of the other types of violence I have discussed, obviously there is more at stake than easing someone's social or psychological burdens. The violence also must be countered, and judgement of and action in relation to that violence is absolutely necessary.

PSYCHOLOGICAL

As I noted in **Chapter 2**, witchcraft and psychiatry are linked historically in the African colonial context. Psychiatry traditionally has pathologised the belief in witchcraft, no matter the cultural context. A more multicultural approach to psychological counselling and support is necessary in dealing with issues such as witchcraft.

Ethnopsychiatry is a newly emerging form of psychiatric practice that deals with cultural phenomena "at face value".[5] Based on innovative practices and methods emanating from the Centre Georges Devereaux at the University of Paris, ethnopsychiatry "focuses on constructing an explanatory narrative, some coherent interpretation of (and then antidote to) the clients' experiences, which have often been invalidated or misunderstood by the various other professionals with whom they have had contact".[6] Therapy relies on multiple practitioners, including Western psychiatrists and folk healers or witch doctors and treats all of their inputs equally. Instead of treating patients for a psychiatric or psychological disorder, ethnopsychiatry treats patients using their own cultural values, referents and sometimes even treatment methods. Kaim states: "setting it apart from much other cultural psychological theory and practice, which sometimes uses cultural sensitivity to facilitate essentially Western treatments, ethnopsychiatry takes the logic of intercultural respect quite seriously, audaciously, all the way to its conclusion".[7]

SPIRITUAL

It is clear that belief in witchcraft has combined syncretically with Christian and other religious beliefs in the African context. Therefore, we must look to how religious and spiritual avenues may be able to provide support in dealing with concerns around and the effects of witchcraft. Some of the African immigrants who have sought support from Cois Tine are looking primarily for spiritual forms of support and sometimes even more practical religious forms of support, in the form of blessings or prayers of protection. One person I spoke with quite extensively discussed the necessity of spiritual awareness and strength to protect oneself against witchcraft. Beyond the role of protection, we can learn much from looking at how spiritual and religious practices can create bridges for better understanding the place of witchcraft in African religious beliefs and practices and for combating the potentially violent effects of witchcraft within the African community in Ireland.

South African Orthodox theologian Stephen Hayes has suggested that we look to the Zionist approach to witchcraft for some strategies for bridging the gap between Western Christian approaches, which generally would be denial of the reality of witchcraft, and African traditional approaches, which would be rooted in the belief in the reality of the power of witchcraft.[8] Zionist Churches, based in South Africa, developed out of the early 20th century missions of the Christian Catholic Apostolic Church and have proliferated into thousands of different congregations throughout South Africa in the last century. Some of the characteristics of Zionist Churches include baptism, faith-healing and dream revelation and many syncretically combine Christian and traditional African practices. The Zionist approach to witchcraft would be to take it seriously but not to engage in witch-hunting or accusations. They are not questioning whether witchcraft exists but are trying to provide ways to defuse its power and restore social harmony in the community. Zionists do this by attempting to convert witches and redeem them, encouraging witches to confess, repent and be reconciled, thus restoring them to the community. According to Hayes, this is currently the most Christian moral point of view at work at the moment.[9]

SOME FINAL THOUGHTS

In this work, I have provided a broad sketch of witchcraft and magic in an attempt to show its embeddedness in African religious, social and cultural beliefs and practices. I began with an examination of witchcraft in the European and Irish contexts, in order to provide the reader with opportunities to draw connections and promote dialogue. I then turned to Africa and looked at how witchcraft has been discussed in the anthropological literature from Evans-Pritchard's seminal work in the 1930s and how that compares to witchcraft practices that are occurring in contemporary Africa. I discussed some of the violent practices associated not only with witchcraft itself but also with its effects, such as trafficking, child accusations, human sacrifice and its association with HIV/AIDs. Finally, I turned to the African experience of witchcraft in Ireland, which was perhaps the most difficult to represent, as it was the section that relied most heavily on anecdotal evidence and confidential communications. In conclusion, I discussed some avenues for thinking about how best to provide African immigrants with the necessary support networks to accommodate their beliefs, promote integration and combat violent practices.

As I mentioned several times throughout this chapter, witchcraft is a difficult subject on many levels but particularly because it is treated as an 'open secret' among the African immigrant community. The community response to the fact that this research was being conducted to some extent has been to close ranks. What does this suggest for possible responses? If we are to provide support and promote integration and inclusion, we must develop ways to understand and interact with non-Western beliefs and practices, by understanding them and drawing connections with our own experiences, to create conditions where people feel comfortable and safe enough to express their concerns, or in some cases violence, so that they can benefit from support services. At the end of the day, it is important to remember that the person you are dealing with is just that – a person, with specific needs and issues, irrespective of their cultural, religious, or societal backgrounds, beliefs or obligations. Make no assumptions, keep an open mind and try to be with the person in their suffering and in their healing.

---

1   Evans-Pritchard, 1976, p. 221.
2   Health Service Executive, 2009, p. 14.
3   Ibid., p. 14.
4   *Ibid.*, pp. 28-29.
5   Kaim, 2008.
6   *Ibid.*
7   *Ibid.*
8   Hayes, 1995.
9   *Ibid.*

PART II
HUMAN TRAFFICKING

No one shall be held in slavery or servitude; slavery and the slave trade shall be prohibited in all their forms.

No one shall be subjected to torture or to cruel, inhuman or degrading treatment or punishment.
Articles 4 and 5, *Universal Declaration of Human Rights*

CHAPTER 5
THE LESSONS OF HISTORY

As Murat Reis peered into the Atlantic darkness of that summer's night, he must have known how very lucky he had been; lucky to survive the aggression of the Ottoman raiders; lucky to be spared the slave markets of Algiers through which many thousands of Europeans had been already sold; and lucky to be recognised by the fellow Dutchman who restored his freedom. Now Reis was back on the water again, in command of his own ship. In the darkness, just out of sight, perched upon a peninsula on the south-west coast of Ireland, lay the small hamlet of Baltimore, County Cork.

With ready access to the waters that have sustained it over its hundreds of years and a sheltered bay, Baltimore is a safe haven for seafarers. The small village stands atop the rolling hills that surround the safety of its bay. From their height, every detail of the bay is visible, making visitors evident long before they present themselves. The contrast between the safety of Baltimore and the peril of Algiers could not have been greater.

Murat Reis was not entirely an innocent party in the tale of his own hardship for, though he had been captured by pirates, he was himself a pirate. At the time of his capture, he had been sailing off North Africa attacking whatever vulnerable vessels he could find and plundering whatever bounty they might be carrying. Whilst sailing near the island of Lanzarote, he had encountered the Barbary Corsairs, a group of pirates even more formidable than his own, and Reis, along with his vessel, was soon their captive.[1] Originally a Dutchman by the name of Jan Janszoon van Haarlem, he had forsaken his past allegiances whilst in captivity and taken the name Murat Reis. Yet it was one of those allegiances that had saved him when a Dutch compatriot, also turned Corsair, secured his freedom. Having cast away so much of his old self, Reis nonetheless returned to his old ways, sailing under a new banner and he was soon commanding the vessels of the Barbary Corsairs.[2] His raiding party now comprised two vessels, one of them a heavily armed 300-ton Dutch-built man-of-war with some 200 men and the other a smaller ship with half the armaments.[3] Reis's past was now behind him; ahead lay Baltimore.

Early on the morning of 20 June 1631, as the residents of Baltimore lay sleeping, the Ottomans disembarked their ships only a short distance away. Making their way quickly and quietly, the raiders were soon at the doors of the 26 sleepy cottages. In the confusion of the opening moments of the raid, two villagers, Thomas Corlew and John Davis, were killed.[4]

When the raiders returned to their ships, they brought with them 107 villagers, consisting of men, women and children. The number of the villagers added to other captives already aboard. This was not an act of piracy consistent with depictions relayed in contemporary films where the bounty is gold and other plunder. The villagers were the intended bounty. The ships set sail for North Africa and the slave markets of Algiers and, as they sailed over the horizon, out of sight of Baltimore, few of the villagers could have held out hope that they would ever see home again. Fewer still could know what awaited them. None were equipped for the journey they were about to make. They did not speak the language of their captors and they did not know their customs. There would be none to whom they could turn for refuge and indeed, if there were, how could they possibly determine where refuge could be found. The different colour of their skin, the difference of their language, their ignorance of local customs and protocols, combined with their lesser standing as mere slaves soon would be sufficient to mark them out as objects of utter contempt.

It is probable that harsh treatment was doled out on the voyage, especially to captive males who were of lesser value than their female counterparts, with the intention of breaking the will of the captives. Special emphasis seems to have been given to harsh punishment in the earliest stages of captivity. More highly prized women and children would have been afforded some kindness.[5] Murray observes that "White women were highly valued and most would have been bought as items of prestige, destined to spend their lives as concubines".[6]

By the time they reached Algiers, a total of 237 captives were aboard, gathered from Baltimore and other engagements. Reis's motives were quite straightforward: he was driven by greed; each captive was but a means to fulfilling his desire for wealth. Remarkably, though the captives had sailed out of sight of Ireland, they had not sailed beyond sight of history. In *Histoire de Barbarie, et de ses corsairs*, the French missionary and Trinitarian priest, Father Pierre Dan, records the plight of the people from a village he thought to be "Batinor" in the slave markets of Algiers.[7] Father Dan laments:

> It was a pitiful thing to see them exposed for sale: for they separated the women from their husbands; & children from their fathers: then I say, they sold the husband on one side, and the wife on the other, snatching her daughter from her arms, without hope of ever meeting again.[8]

Father Dan adds that there were many tears shed by onlookers and that it was a matter of extreme regret to see so many decent persons abandoned to the brutality of barbarians.[9] Even in the 17th century, efforts were being made to alleviate the suffering of those who found themselves the victim of inhumane circumstance. A Reverend Devereux Spratt who:

> ... was captured off Youghal as he was crossing on leave from Cork to Bristol, and so distressed was the good man at the miserable condition of many of the slaves at Algiers, that when he was ransomed he yielded to their entreaties and stayed a year or two longer to comfort them with his holy offices.[10]

It is worth noting that, at this time, the Ottomans did not have a monopoly on this form of tyranny: "European seafaring powers engaged equally in ... the use of ... slave labour. In addition, the European trade in African slaves [was at this time] ... beginning to increase in volume and efficiency".[11]

History does not record the financial reward Reis received for his efforts and it records little of what subsequently happened to the captives of Baltimore. There are some suggestions that a small few may have returned to Europe.[12] What is remarkable is how many similarities there are between the account of what happened to the people of Baltimore in 1631 and what happens today to those sold into slavery through human trafficking. Yet, in other regards, much has changed with regard to our understanding of the phenomenon. The body of knowledge concerning human slavery, or human trafficking as it is referred to nowadays, has grown considerably and extensive research is now possible. The materials consist of books, newspaper articles, peer-reviewed journal articles, conference proceedings, documentaries, online materials and expert reports by international bodies, governments, policing authorities, other authorities and non-governmental organisations. The methodology used in the preparation of this publication draws upon an analysis of all of the aforementioned and combines them with case studies and interviews to provide an extensive account of human trafficking.

Contemporary research methods can determine, for example, how Reis would have fared in today's slave markets. If Reis was selling a woman in Eastern Europe, he could expect to receive a price of between US$2,500 and US$7,000.[13] Were he to sell a child in the United Kingdom, he might expect to receive Stg£16,000, whereas in Iran the price would be just US$5.[14] That same child, sold in post-earthquake Haiti, would earn Reis just €0.90.[15] In Nigeria, infant boys cost more than infant girls: US$3,875 and US$2,325 respectively.[16] There may be good cause as to why such information is available for women and children; just as in the days of the Algerian slave markets, they remain today prized commodities. Those same research methods also can determine that Reis would no longer need to transport his victims to far-away Algiers. He could instead sell them in practically any European country, including Ireland. The *Trafficking in Persons Report* describes Ireland in 2011 as "a destination ... country for women, men, and children subjected to sex trafficking and forced labor".[17]

Much though can be learned from history. Slavery is an age-old problem and a practice that inflicts immeasurable misery on those upon whom it preys. It is also a practice closely associated with financial reward and its existence threatens all persons, wherever they may be. The people of Baltimore may have been oblivious to the impending danger posed to them by the slave markets of Algiers, considering it a far-off problem of little relevance to their place. Alas, even in the 1600s, the far-flung troubles of the world could be visited upon an unsuspecting community. Today, the world is a much more complex place where sophisticated trade routes exist, people communicate in real-time though they are separated by immense distances and those same distances may be traversed in mere hours. Greater opportunities exist for criminal fraternities to impose exploitative methods, hitherto only visited upon their locality, on a broader community.

---

1   Wilson, 2003, p. 96.
2   *Ibid.*, p. 97.
3   Murray, 2006, p. 15.
4   *Ibid.*, p. 16.
5   *Ibid.*, p. 17.
6   *Ibid.*, p. 18.
7   Dan, 1649, p. 315.
8   *Ibid.*, p. 315. Translated by the author.
9   *Ibid.*, p. 315.
10   Lane-Poole and Kelley, 1970, p. 266.
11   Murray, 2006, p. 15.
12   Baltimore Heritage Limited, n.d.
13   Lee, 2007, p. 102.

14 BBC News (UK), 2011b; United States Department of State, 2011, p. 195.

15 Gammelli, 2011.

16 UNESCO, 2006, p. 31.

17 United States Department of State, 2011, p. 198.

CHAPTER 6
CASE STUDY 1:
THE SNEEP CASE

Ireland, Holland and Turkey (the successors to the Ottomans) form a nexus whose relationship to one another on the issue of human trafficking has been an unhappy affair. One can point to the sack of Baltimore for its origins. But history has a way of repeating itself, sometimes partially and sometimes entirely so.

Human trafficking is a problem in Holland, where prostitution has been legalised for over a decade. Dutch Public Prosecutor Inge Schepers describes how the lifting of the ban on brothels was supposed to normalise prostitution and to improve practices within Holland's sex industry but the very thing society sought to improve was made manifestly worse through its actions.[1] The 2010 report of the Dutch National Rapporteur on Trafficking Human Beings concedes:

> There has always been a clear relationship between human trafficking and prostitution in the Netherlands. Human trafficking has been associated with prostitution ever since it was included in Dutch criminal law.[2]

In the ten years 2000 to 2009, Dutch authorities recorded 5,084 victims of human trafficking.[3] Of these 5,084 victims, it can be established that, between the years 2006 to 2009 inclusive, 582 victims were encountered who were categorised as "underage" when located.[4] As is the case with all criminal activities, the figures reflect only part of the reality. The true figures necessarily must be higher than those detailed here.

In the 2005 report of the Dutch National Rapporteur, it was revealed that an Irish citizen had likely been trafficked in Holland just two years prior.[5] This case may be the first recorded instance of an Irish citizen being trafficked into forced commercial sexual exploitation in contemporary times. Any uncertainty surrounding the allegation has evaporated in the intervening years and subsequent reports by the Dutch National Rapporteur have recorded the event as an instance of human trafficking.[6]

History repeated itself only a short time later. This time, all parties to the nexus of Ireland, Holland and Turkey once again were involved when Holland's most high-profile and notorious case of human trafficking emerged. In what would become known as the 'Sneep case', over 120 women, mostly women from Eastern Europe and Holland, were trafficked for forced commercial sexual exploitation by a Turkish gang.[7] There are several remarkable aspects to the case. Of particular interest to Ireland is the fact that an Irish citizen was one of those trafficked into forced commercial sexual exploitation.[8]

The original complaint that led to the Sneep case was made in 1998 and investigations were conducted in 2000 and again in 2003.[9] A further complaint was made thereafter but it was only in 2007, almost 10 years after the original complaint was made, that the first arrests were made.[10] As a single case, the scale of the crime was also staggering. To put the figure of 120 victims into some context, it represents almost 150% of the total number of victims encountered in the Republic of Ireland during 2010.[11]

Some may consider the most remarkable aspect of the Sneep case to be the fact that the victims were openly prostituted *via* licensed window prostitution.[12] Indeed, the Dutch National Rapporteur on Human Beings recognises that situations "of human trafficking are not always easy to recognise".[13] It may seem extraordinary that so many adults could be so effectively enslaved in such a public space over a long period of time and be forced to engage in commercial sex work. Yet, there is no reason to suppose that human trafficking in Holland's public places was a unique event and that other cases have been confined to more secluded spaces. "Amsterdam has registered the largest number of human trafficking cases in the nine year period" 2000 to 2009, a figure of 197 victims in all.[14]

If victims can be so publicly found in Holland, it compels the question of where else they might be found and how they might be identified. The answer lies with the starting point. The starting point in human trafficking always must lie with the role of violence, which is always much more than mere contempt for the victim or general opportunism on the part of the trafficker. This is not to say that these are not factors but rather that violence plays another role too, one much larger than may be appreciated initially. It plays a role capable of explaining how 120 victims of human trafficking can be left on public display for a decade in circumstances where they are sexually exploited several times daily.

---

[1]   Schepers, 2011.

[2]   National Rapporteur on Trafficking in Human Beings, 2010, p. 26.

[3]   *Ibid.*, p. 167.

[4]   *Ibid.*, p. 169.

[5]   Korvinus *et al.*, 2005, p. 47.

[6]   National Rapporteur on Trafficking in Human Beings, 2010, p. 162.

[7]   United States Department of State, 2011, p. 273; Siegel, 2009, p. 9.

[8]   Korps landelijke politiediensten, 2008, p. 11; Schepers, 2011; Aronowitz, 2009, p. 69.

[9]   National Rapporteur on Trafficking in Human Beings, 2010, p. 64.

[10] *Ibid.*, p. 64.

[11] Anti-Human Trafficking Unit, 2011.

[12] Siegel, 2009, p. 9; Schepers, 2011.

[13] National Rapporteur on Trafficking in Human Beings, 2010, p. 65.

[14] *Ibid.*, p. 116.

CHAPTER 7
VIOLENCE AND VICTIMHOOD

The International Organization for Migration (IOM) has said that "Trafficking should be seen as a process, starting with the recruitment and ending with the exploitation".[1] The word "process" is an intriguing one for IOM to have used, especially when one considers the many places where trafficking occurs and the many peoples who fall prey to traffickers. Traffickers do not collaborate as a worldwide group, so how can the act of trafficking in one part of the world have much in common with that in another? How can it be described as a "process"?

The reading of an individual account of the experiences of a victim certainly would not lead the reader to believe that there was any kind of process involved. At best, the poor unfortunate victim would appear to have endured unimaginable repeated exploitation at the hands of opportunists. However, with the reading of the stories of several victims, certain words seem to reoccur with almost tragic predictability and, gradually, particular themes become evident. As they emerge, these themes make it clear that IOM's assertion that trafficking should be viewed as a process is entirely appropriate. The essence of the trafficking process is one in which the victim at every stage is losing power, while the trafficker increasingly obtains more control over the victim. At the end of this process, the victim will have no power whatsoever, even over the most fundamental decisions affecting their own self. The reader is advised to observe not only *what is done*, but also *why it is done*.

There are several reasons too for looking at human trafficking, as IOM advises, "starting with the recruitment and ending with the exploitation".[2] Firstly, this method, which I call a process-based approach, puts the victim centre-stage, prioritising his or her situation and needs; everything else becomes a secondary consideration. Foremost in such an approach is an attempt to understand the impact of the process of trafficking on the victim and thereafter to anticipate the needs of victims. Secondly, this victim-centred approach permits the profiling of likely victims of trafficking in which seemingly insignificant details, when pieced together, take on greater meaning. This can be an important element in trying to identify victims of trafficking for the purpose of assisting those still under the control of traffickers. Thirdly, the process-based approach is useful in trying to understand what human trafficking actually is. Can human trafficking be defined? What is a useful definition? A variety of perspectives are available but this is the only one that looks at trafficking as the victim has experienced it. Finally, this is probably the only such approach that can reveal trafficking for the abhorrent violation of human dignity and of the human being that it truly is.

RECRUITMENT

Most of those who set out on the pathway that eventually leads to their exploitation do so in the simple and very human desire for "a better life".[3] In these times of global economic uncertainty, it is much easier to relate to the tale recorded in the many accounts of past victims, that of "individuals seeking to escape from dire economic circumstances".[4] This is the same tale that continually feeds the supply of unsuspecting victims. It is a fact that victims of human trafficking "are usually those most disadvantaged in their own countries: those with poor job skills or little chance of successful employment at home. They are often women and children".[5]

The process begins with recruitment. Remember for a moment the excitement and sheer joy upon learning that you had been successful in getting your first-ever job. Looking back on it, such events are landmarks, fantastic achievements in our lives and moments that show how important success can be. These are simple pleasures; the desire only for the opportunity to improve oneself, to provide for oneself and for one's family. Yet for a trafficker, such simple desires represent something else entirely; they represent vulnerability and, wherever vulnerability is present, it can be exploited. There are various strategies used by recruiters: the offer of a job is an approach commonly used.[6] There is also the practice of the "so-called 'lover-boy' recruitment mode whereby a man (often a foreigner)" seduces his prospective victim with promises of a future together, one that includes an offer of marriage.[7] Both strategies are consistent with an understanding of the desire by human beings to improve their lives and escape prevailing hardship. By way of example:

> *Skaffari and Urponen (2004, 42) note that young Russian women often dream of going abroad. Young women are promised jobs in beauty parlours or office jobs and a reasonable living. These women are easily persuaded to leave their home country.*[8]

While the main strategies consist of the offer of employment or that of marriage, the tactics used are slightly more varied. Offers concerning marriage are largely self-explanatory; offers relating to employment may come from "partners, or members of" the victim's own wider family;[9] many are the result of "false advertisements", whether on billboard posters, in newspapers, on radio or television.[10] Recruitment methods can be quite sophisticated, complete with genuine-looking contracts. Some Eastern European gangs have even gone as far as organising recruitment fairs.[11] Sometimes, even the very smallest of details regarding travel, employment and income are minutely described to add to the deception.[12] Of course, none of these offers by recruiters are genuine. One of the key aspects of human trafficking, especially at this stage, is the role of deception:[13]

Alexandra, an inmate at Neve Tirza, Israel's only women's prison, was initially recruited when she "responded to an ad on cable television for girls between the ages of 18 and 35 to work abroad as models, masseuses and waitresses". Once in Israel, she was sold to the owner of a brothel.[14]

Depictions of human trafficking most famously portray it as kidnapping. While kidnappings do happen, it would be best not to rely on them for one's primary understanding of human trafficking. For example, in places, parents have actively engaged in, and continue to engage in, the sale of their children, and families in the sale of female members.[15] However, deception is much more frequently employed as it is a subtle coercive power that has proven most efficient in the process of trafficking persons. On occasion, some who become embroiled in human trafficking may be aware that "they are being recruited into the sex industry ... but are deceived about their conditions of work".[16] Overall, victims made compliant through deception are more easily managed than those forced through kidnapping.

In the eyes of the victim, the trafficker, acting as a recruiter, appears to have the power to solve their problems and lead them to a new and better life. Through the outwardly appearing kindness of their offer of help, the targeted person may feel indebted by gratitude. It may seem extraordinary in some regards that control over a person may be exerted by such subtle means but this is the very nature by which the process can start. Predictably enough, as the victim is most often trying to escape economic hardship, they are unlikely to have the funds required to make the journey or to pay for travel documents. This is a predicament entirely anticipated by traffickers and one they are only too willing to exploit. When the matter of money arises, it is the trafficker who offers to pay the victim's way thus imposing a debt upon their prey.

THE BONDAGE OF DEBT

The debts incurred can be very substantial, even by Western standards. Some Nigerians have owed as much as €60,000 and the perception is that they will have to work "for a while" to reimburse the trafficker.[17] Sr. Monica Onwunali of The Congregation of Sisters of Our Lady of Apostles (OLA) works in Rome with Unione Superiore Maggiori d'Italia (USMI) to combat human trafficking. In an interview, Sr. Onwunali explained that, in Nigeria, good jobs pay at least 50,000 Nigerian Naira (NGN) each month.[18] This equates to approximately US$320. Sr. Onwunali notes that one must bear in mind that these are largely uneducated girls with no knowledge of the concept of money markets and the consequential international currency conversion. Some of these girls will never have gone to school. So, when Nigerian girls are told that they will have debts of €50,000, the logic then is quite simple from their perspective: if a good job in Nigeria can pay 50,000 Nigerian Naira (NGN) each month, then surely a good job in the West can pay €50,000 (approx. US$67,000) per month. After all, 50,000 equals 50,000, doesn't it?

By making an offer to fund the expenses of the victim, an arrangement that requires the repayment of the debt later on, the victim has been placed in a situation of debt bondage.[19] Far from being an example of a compassionate act, it is an entirely exploitative arrangement, though this is likely not appreciated by the victim:

> Debt bondage occurs when traffickers provide their victims with a loan under agreement that it will be repaid with the money earned in the destination country. However, this loan is usually so high that repayment is impossible or will take years to pay off.[20]

The practice of debt bondage is criminalised under international agreements as a form of human trafficking. Its real purpose is to place the victim in a position where the debt can be unlawfully exploited.[21] The plausible manner in which such an illegal pact can be proposed and accepted is another example of the subtle nature of the coercive forces being gathered by the trafficker and the ever-diminishing autonomy of the victim.

WITCHCRAFT

Another form of coercion which, when presented in the context of culture can seem entirely fair and normal, is the use of supernatural power, witchcraft or magic. These span a wide variety of beliefs and practices, which in some parts of Africa are more specifically referred to as Voodoo or Juju. In the case of African victims of human trafficking, practices such as Voodoo or Juju may be used as a spiritual, or psychological, hold upon the person. Why would someone agree to this arrangement? On the face of it, the answer seems quite simple. From the victim's perspective, their inability to pay their own way has placed the recruiter in a position where the recruiter has to cover the full expense of the journey to be made. Naturally, the recruiter will want his money returned and the use of an oath to assure the recruiter must seem reasonable. After all, how could the recruiter possibly benefit from non-payment of the debt? The reality though is that recruiters do benefit from non-payment because it assures ongoing control and compliance. The victim has placed themselves in a position of spiritual checkmate. They have agreed to be bound to their recruiter by the terms of a financial agreement, under penalty of spiritual sanction, that they really have no prospect of ever paying. Oaths also may be used to assure confidentiality.[22]

At this point, the enormity of the power held by the recruiter-trafficker is becoming apparent and, all the while, the victim is losing more and more capacity for self-help. The United Nations body UNESCO has noted that witchcraft adds a layer of complexity into the issue of human trafficking where Africans are concerned.[23] A report by the Swedish Police observes that African witchcraft compels victims to:

... believe that some sort of misfortune will happen to them or their family if they break their promises by not doing what they are told.[24]

Witchcraft is being used in Ireland. The Irish Anti-Human Trafficking Unit (AHTU) has reported that 13% of the human trafficking victims surveyed over a two-year period had been coerced by Juju.[25] Some adjustment of the figure is warranted though, as almost 27% of those surveyed were not from African countries. The figure climbs to 18% when one restates the figure in the context of African countries.[26] It is likely that it would be even higher in relation to the victims of particular African countries where the practice is widely used, though published figures do not permit this level of scrutiny, which may be entirely consistent with an approach that respects the privacy of victims.

As noted in **Part One**, the significance of witchcraft, and indeed the respectful treatment of those who fall prey to it, should not be dismissed. That one may, or may not, subscribe to belief in it is of little relevance to the victim who does. The seriousness of witchcraft is implicitly acknowledged in the U.S. Government's *Trafficking in Persons Report 2011*, which recognises the efforts of "German federal criminal police [in providing] a series of seminars on ... Voodoo rituals".[27] The seriousness of the matter is more explicitly acknowledged in the case of France where "trafficking networks controlled by Bulgarians, Romanians, Nigerians, and French citizens force women into prostitution through ... the invocation of Voodoo".[28] A Swedish police report observes the lessons learnt by German authorities, specifically that "the first step in contact with women who have been exposed to controlling Voodoo rituals is to show acceptance", thus "it is only when confidence has been built up that women talk about what they have gone through".[29]

TRAVEL

More weight ought to be placed on what can happen during travel rather than on the fact that travel has occurred. *En route* to the final destination, a number of countries may be visited and a variety of "modes of transport used".[30] In an attempt to avoid detection by immigration officials, indirect routes may be taken to the final destinations. One victim from Thailand started out "in a hotel in Bangkok for three days", from which she travelled to Brunei and later on to Abu Dhabi.[31] She recalls that thereafter she was flown from Abu Dhabi to Dublin, where she took a train to Belfast and then she was transported to England.[32] Once in London, she was transported to a flat where she encountered seven or eight other girls, who British police suspected were also victims of trafficking.[33] Soon after, she was sold, after some bargaining, for Stg£30,000.[34]

The indirect route also may reflect the involvement of other persons in the trafficking process and victims may be passed from one trafficker to another along the route. Victims located in Ireland subsequently recalled "being transported by plane, train, bus, car and boat ferry" and combinations thereof.[35]

It is a common feature of trafficking that victims eventually end up without their travel documents, including passports and any visas they may require.[36] Some documents may have been forged and retained by the trafficker upon arrival. A further source of power then may be the illegality of the presence of the victim in the country, though this is not always necessarily the case: "trafficked people frequently enter the state legally".[37] For those visiting illegally, not only is the trafficker in possession of their travel documents but, if the trafficker were to renounce the victim to the authorities, they would be virtually helpless against deportation proceedings.[38] Rescue can bring its own problems, as the rescued slave may end up in jail for violating immigration and other laws. Additionally, most "countries summarily deport rescued slaves".[39] In this context, some commentators maintain that "the State response is complicit with the interests of the trafficker and strengthens the position of the trafficker".[40]

ARRIVAL, ABUSE AND ISOLATION

Events can unfold in many different ways. Some victims may be sold immediately upon arrival;[41] for others, this may occur later on or even not at all. Whatever may happen in this regard, one particular fate awaits many and the day comes when they are "put into a room and effectively expected to work as prostitutes".[42] The victim will soon be having sex with many men each day and suffer "sexual assault at the hands of not only their traffickers but also ... [the trafficker's] clients".[43]

Other victims are not forced immediately into prostitution. Instead, they are advised that there has been a problem in providing the promised job and it is no longer available. Victims then are put to work doing some menial tasks for which they are paid a trivial amount. Their indebtedness takes on new meaning as the realisation dawns that the low pay of the assigned duties could never hope to repay the enormous debt that forms part of the arrangement. They need not arrive at the realisation concerning the problem with their debt themselves, as the trafficker will be only too happy to remind them of it, repeatedly, and to use it as a means to abuse their self-worth.

Verbal abuse is often used.[44] Demeaning the person serves a deliberate purpose, undermining self-confidence and undermining the very dignity of those demeaned and emphasising the lesser position occupied. This is all part of the well-planned ploy on the part of the trafficker who uses every aspect of self-doubt and guilt as leverage to gain more control. All the while, the victim is crumbling under a constant barrage of ever-emerging crises and beginning to feel quite powerless over the forces guiding his or her life. At this juncture, the realisation also must be dawning about how very different their future prospects are beginning to appear from the ones that first motivated them to leave the safety of their families, friends, communities and countries.

However, these are not the only psychological weapons used by traffickers. Many victims are threatened and live with the fear this entails.[45] Traffickers also have learned the potency of another form of threatening behaviour which, judging by the frequency with which it is used, they find particularly effective. Threats are made against family members back home, far from where the victim can do anything to protect them or even know whether they have been harmed;[46] one victim was told that "she would not see her child again if she did not pay back the debt created from her travelling and visa expenses".[47] This is a particularly vicious form of psychological violence, as it seems to emphasise just how far-removed one is from the safety of one's family and from control over one's own life.

Violence is not limited to these kinds of activities. Physical violence is employed also and victims "are often subject[ed] to physical beatings".[48] Even starvation has been used in some cases.[49] Alcohol and drugs also may be used to assure compliance.[50]

The most dreadful form of violence that might be employed is that of sexual assault. Sexual abuse is an immeasurable crisis in the life of a person. For victims of trafficking, rape becomes just one of many crises they are forced to endure and it is endured in the midst of so many others.[51] For the trafficker, sexual assault is just another weapon to be used. To view the act as being solely rooted in contempt or opportunism would be to miss the point. There is a much colder and sinister element to the act that makes it an almost inevitable occurrence. Rape in human trafficking is a weapon because it enables victims to be "raped into acquiescence".[52]

Another form of abuse imposed is isolation. A seemingly unrelated manifestation of this is the deliberate practice of withholding wages.[53] Persons engaged in forced sexual commercial exploitation must collect monies from clients for the madams or pimps who control them. These madams and others associated with the trafficking process deliberately withhold wages or use the withholding of wages as a punitive measure when the victim has incurred their wrath. One such example given in a report from Finland of conditions under which wages are withheld is "if the woman did not inform beforehand about her menstruation period" thus leaving her unavailable to work.[54]

A further ploy used is the levying of charges. Sr. Onwunali has encountered this problem in the course of her work in Italy. She has observed how sex workers are further coerced in relation to their debt by the addition of other expenses purportedly incurred by their madam.[55] For example, the initial debt incurred by the victims in bringing them into the country will not include the bed they sleep in, the water they drink and, as she notes, even the ground where they stand to offer sex services must be rented from the madam. Small wonder then that Sr. Monica concludes that the victims "have failed to realise that they will never come out of it ... The madam's demands are endless". The overall effect is to deny the victim any form of independence and to foster dependence, thus exacerbating their situation of isolation.

Another significant factor in isolating victims, evident in many reports, is the role of language.[56] Quite simply, the victim is in a foreign country, perhaps even a country that they had not expected to be in, with little or no command of the local language. Imagine for a moment how very quickly someone becomes isolated from the mainstream, even as a tourist to a foreign country, when one does not speak the language, the signs are in unintelligible script, the symbols mean nothing and one does not presume to afford the authorities the same level of trust one might in one's own country. How many readers would know how to say "No" in the languages of Eastern Europe, Africa or the Philippines? Yet these are the very peoples trafficked into Ireland and abused in brothels here; it seems probable that they have little capacity to say "No" either.[57] According to the United Nations:

A lack of knowledge of ... cultural and linguistic obstacles ...
combine to further isolate trafficked women and to prevent them
from seeking or receiving justice.[58]

The factual nature of this United Nations statement seems to
contrast against the harsh reality of 17 year old Marinella, who did
not know even how to say "No" in English when she was
kidnapped and trafficked from Romania to a brothel in Manchester,
where she was "raped by different men 50 times a week on
average".[59] Journalist Mark Townsend conveys Marinella's
recollection of her experience:

When the first 'client' booked her she wanted to say "No" but could
not. She wanted to explain her predicament, tell the man that she
was trafficked. Instead she cried, hoping that the man would take
pity on her. He did not. None of them did.[60]

There is evidence to show that traffickers fully understand the
importance the absence of language skills can play. One report by
the Migrant Rights Centre Ireland (MRCI) provided an example of
an employer who travelled to the Ukraine to handpick prospective
employees he would engage in conditions of forced labour. This
employer had a particular preference for those Ukrainians who had
little or no English. Indeed, workers who possessed a good
command of the language were not considered suitable
candidates.[61]

In reflecting on the predicament of the victim, it is worth noting
that the exact placement of where and when the various forms of
abuse occur, or indeed their frequency, is not possible and it is
unnecessary. One study of female victims showed half had been
"confined, raped or beaten during the travel and transit stage".[62]
The trafficking process is better understood in terms of an erosion
of autonomy than as a strict step-by-step process used by
traffickers. In reporting on a series of cases in which young girls
were abused in the United Kingdom, reporter Andrew Norfolk was

aware that the abusers created "what they sought: compliant human beings to be traded and abused".[63]

COMPLIANCE AND EXPLOITATION

There is, by this stage, good cause for compliance on the part of the victim. Consider for a moment her plight. The victim is probably far from home, perhaps in a foreign country, likely without possession of travel documents, isolated by the fact that she may understand neither the culture nor the language or everyday signs advertising assistance. Added to this, she may have little cause to trust the authorities based on her experiences at home. Instead she is indebted to a person who exploits her, who may have bound her by the rites of witchcraft, who has likely abused her, who threatens her and her family and who, at any time, could choose to renounce her to the authorities who in turn may well imprison and thereafter deport her.

In ruling on a particular case in Australia, Justice McInerney described the facts of the case before him thus:

> How could they run away when they had no money, they had no passport or ticket, they entered on an illegally obtained visa, albeit legal on its face, they had limited English language, they had no friends, they were told to avoid Immigration, they had come to Australia consensually to earn income and were aware of the need to work particularly hard in order to pay off a debt of approximately $45,000 before they were able to earn income for themselves?[64]

When someone claims that they are under the influence or control of another, it might now be possible to understand how this could well be so. Accordingly, this raises questions about the commonly-held preconceptions concerning 'consenting adults' and perhaps stereotypical imagery of victims shackled to beds. The U.S. Dept of State has called for a more:

... sophisticated understanding of the realities on the ground ... to ensure that ... trafficking victims are not wrongly discounted as consenting adults.[65]

Once the difficult task of gaining compliance has been achieved, the exploitation or use of the person for the purpose intended is comparatively straightforward. Having arrived at the point of exploitation, the process of trafficking, one "starting with the recruitment and ending with the exploitation", is completed, though the enslavement continues.[66] While particular attention has been given in this instance to the process as it applies to forced commercial sexual exploitation, parallels may be readily drawn with other forms of exploitation such as forced labour or even human trafficking for organ transplantation. Just as is the case with sexual exploitation, the process where the power of trafficker increases while that of the victim diminishes is, albeit in different circumstances, the same.

UNDERSTANDING 'WHAT?' AND 'WHY?'

One of the objectives stated earlier was an appreciation of both *what is done* and of *why it is done* in the process of trafficking persons. The former consideration is mindful of the abuse endured by the victim, primarily to gain an understanding of the violence endured and to permit the consequences, in all their guises, to be addressed. The latter consideration seeks to see the process from the perspective of the trafficker, to understand the role of power in trafficking and the manner in which it is used to fulfil the selfish ends of the trafficker. Paradoxically, through an understanding of *why it is done*, the *what is done* becomes predictable; the objective is power over the individual and the means towards that objective are achieved through any action that undermines the autonomy of the person and continually contributes to such an undermining. It is small wonder then that, even in the absence of global co-ordination of trafficking practices, Síle Nic Gabhan observes:

There is ample recorded evidence to indicate that the methods of recruitment and entrapment used by traffickers are similar worldwide.[67]

A claim made in this chapter relates to the emergence of particular themes throughout various unrelated accounts of trafficking and the significance of particular words. This account is given in the hope that the reader will now look at even the briefest of accounts, identify particular words and appreciate, more fully, their significance:

In June 2009 Murariu invited her to the UK. He bought the bus ticket as a 'gift' for her, and they travelled together from Romania to London. Upon arrival he took her to a house in Hendon Way, north west London. Just three days into the trip she was raped ... Murariu forced her into prostitution, selling her body for sex to repay the debt for transporting her to the UK. She was threatened by Murariu; he insisted that if she did not perform sexual acts for money, he would lie to her family, claiming she was uncontrollable, working as a prostitute out of choice.[68]

Detachment may be possible for the observer. It is certainly a necessity to analyse what is being done to the person and to comprehend why it is being done. Bearing in mind that if detachment is necessary for analysis, then the victims themselves may not be capable of grasping why they have been so ill-treated. Indeed, there may be little cause to suppose that many who fall victim to the practice of human trafficking have heard of it or even know what it is. Instead, the effects and memories of what has been done may be all-consuming. In the (translated) words of the Thai victim who was mentioned earlier and had been trafficked through Ireland to the United Kingdom, she describes her ordeal thus:

I envy the dogs in this country. People love them and take such good care of them. These people treated me worse than an animal. They sold me like a pig ... [69]

The words of this victim contrast against a terrible realisation that neither she nor any other person will ever be treated otherwise by a trafficker.

Trafficking is a process, one that uses power to exploit the vulnerability of persons for its own selfish ends. With this realisation comes another: trafficking is not a story told or indeed a story being told, trafficking is a story yet to be told. The sexual and other abuse of, predominantly, women and children will continue to occur through their exploitation by traffickers unless the issue is addressed. Their tales can be mapped out clinically, often coldly, as has been done here, to gain an understanding of the phenomenon but it behoves us to appreciate, in the words of Cois Tine Director, Fr. Angelo Lafferty SMA, that "there is a reality other than our own" and for millions, this is theirs.

---

[1]   International Organization for Migration (IOM), n.d.

[2]   *Ibid.*

[3]   *Irish Examiner*, 2011; Viuhko and Jokinen, 2009, p. 13; Buckley, 2004, p. 30; *Al Jazeera*, 2011.

[4]   Stone and Vandenberg, 1999, p. 36.

[5]   Aronowitz, 2001, p. 167.

[6]   Siegel, 2009, p. 7; Olaniyi, 2003, p. 48; Rogers, 2011b; Nic Gabhan, 2006, p. 530; Cole, 2006, p. 219; Goodey, 2004, p. 28; Viuhko and Jokinen, 2009, p. 27.

[7]   Lee, 2007, p. 100.

[8]   Viuhko and Jokinen, 2009, p. 47.

[9]   Ruhama, n.d.

[10] Stone and Vandenberg, 1999, p. 37.

[11] Siegel, 2009, p. 7.

[12] Lee, 2007, p. 101.

[13] United Nations Office on Drugs and Crime, n.d.; Aronowitz, 2001, p. 166; Kelleher *et al.*, 2009, p. 1; Viuhko and Jokinen, 2009, p. 50.

[14] Stone and Vandenberg, 1999, p. 37.

[15] Nic Gabhan, 2006, p. 530; Gammelli, 2011.

[16] United Nations, 2001.

[17] Lally, 2010b.

18 Interview given September 2011.
19 Buckley, 2004, p. 30; Anti-Human Trafficking Unit, 2011, p. 49; Cole, 2006, p. 217; Department of Justice, Equality & Law Reform, n.d., p. 29.
20 Department of Justice, Equality & Law Reform, n.d., p. 29.
21 United States Department of State, 2011, pp. 7-8.
22 Cole, 2006, p. 222.
23 UNESCO, 2006, p. 36.
24 Polisen, 2010, p. 12.
25 Anti-Human Trafficking Unit, 2011, p. 49.
26 *Ibid.*, p. 49.
27 United States Department of State, 2011, p. 170.
28 *Ibid.*, p. 163.
29 Polisen, 2010, p. 12.
30 Aronowitz, 2001, p. 175.
31 Channel 4, 2010b.
32 Channel 4, 2010a.
33 Channel 4, 2010b.
34 Channel 4, 2010a.
35 Kelleher *et al.*, 2009, p. 22.
36 *Ibid.*, p. 54; Buckley, 2004, p. 30; Miller, 2008, p. 52.
37 Migrant Rights Centre Ireland, 2006, p. 21.
38 Goodey, 2004, p. 38.
39 Miller, 2008, p. 56.
40 Kelleher *et al.*, 2009, p. 22.
41 London Metropolitan Police Service, 2010.
42 Rogers, 2011b.
43 Nam, 2007, p. 1685.
44 Department of Justice, Equality & Law Reform, n.d., p. 29.
45 O'Brien, 2009; Brison, 2006, p. 195; Haynes, 2004, p. 270; Kapstein, 2006, p. 106; National Rapporteur on Trafficking in Human Beings, 2010, p. 82; Townsend, 2011.
46 Rogers, 2011b; Goodey, 2004, p. 39; Kapstein, 2006, p. 106; Department of Justice, Equality & Law Reform, n.d., p. 29.
47 Viuhko & Jokinen, 2009, p. 52.
48 Nam, 2007, p. 1685.
49 Olaniyi, 2003, p. 50; Anti-Human Trafficking Unit, 2011, p. 49.
50 Norfolk, 2011; *The Times*, 2011; Department of Justice, Equality & Law Reform, n.d., p. 228; Anti-Human Trafficking Unit, 2011, p. 49.

51   Nam, 2007, p. 1685; Remensnyder *et al.*, 2005, p. 19; London Metropolitan Police Service, 2010; United States Department of Health & Human Services, n.d.; Burkhalter, 2004, p. 2.

52   Olaniyi, 2003, p. 50.

53   Anti-Human Trafficking Unit, 2011, p. 49.

54   Viuhko and Jokinen, 2009, p. 27.

55   Interview given September 2011.

56   Goodey, 2004, p. 28; Miller, 2008, p. 55; Buckley, 2004, p. 31; Organization for Security and Co-operation in Europe (OSCE), n.d., p. 1.

57   United States Department of State, 2011, p. 198.

58   United Nations, 2001.

59   Townsend, 2011.

60   *Ibid.*

61   Migrant Rights Centre Ireland, 2006, p. 14.

62   Burkhalter, 2004, p. 2.

63   Norfolk, 2011.

64   Quoted in David, 2008, p. 54.

65   United States Department of State, 2011, p. 24.

66   International Organization for Migration (IOM), n.d.

67   Nic Gabhan, 2006, p. 530.

68   London Metropolitan Police Service, 2010.

69   Channel 4, 2010b.

CHAPTER 8
THE *PALERMO PROTOCOL*

A process-based approach to human trafficking has advantages, some previously mentioned. It permits an appreciation of the kinds of exploitation endured by victims. Armed with this understanding, predictions can be made about the needs and care of victims. Additionally, the approach is useful in trying to convey to others what trafficking is. This is a fairly large consideration in light of the number and enormity of the forces (for example, the United Nations, European Union, OSCE, U.S. Department of State, national governments, etc.) gathered to combat the issue. There is little point in trying to discuss a concept if everybody understands it in different terms.

In 2000, the United Nations managed to reach agreement on a definition that identifies three critical components to human trafficking: the act, the means and the purpose.[1] An act includes actions such as "recruitment, transportation, transfer, harbouring or receipt of persons". The means include using "threat or use of force, coercion, abduction, fraud, deception, abuse of power or vulnerability, or giving payments or benefits". The purpose is predominantly one of exploitation, including "prostitution of others, sexual exploitation, forced labour, slavery or similar practices, removal of organs or other types of exploitation".[2]

The *United Nations Convention against Transnational Organized Crime* was signed in Palermo, Italy,[3] supplemented by two protocols: the *Protocol to Prevent, Suppress and Punish Trafficking in Persons, Especially Women and Children* and the *Protocol against the Smuggling of Migrants by Land, Sea and Air.* The first of these protocols is sometimes referred to as the *Trafficking Protocol* and more usually as the *Palermo Protocol.*

The definition provided in the *Palermo Protocol* defines human trafficking thus:

'Trafficking in persons' shall mean the recruitment, transportation, transfer, harbouring or receipt of persons, by means of the threat or use of force or other forms of coercion, of abduction, of fraud, of deception, of the abuse of power or of a position of vulnerability or of the giving or receiving of payments or benefits to achieve the consent of a person having control over another person, for the purpose of exploitation. Exploitation shall include, at a minimum, the exploitation of the prostitution of others or other forms of sexual exploitation, forced labour or services, slavery or practices similar to slavery, servitude or the removal of organs.[4]

Revisiting the process-based approach explored earlier, it is easy to understand how the United Nations reached this common definition, whose significance is that it is the very first internationally-agreed definition of human trafficking.[5]

Several points may be observed from the definition. There is no mention of borders. Trafficking does not require transportation across borders. Trafficking can be internal to a country, which is sometimes referred to as internal trafficking.[6] "Ninety percent of trafficking in India is internal" and this in a country where trafficking is a huge problem.[7] In Senegal too, trafficking "within the country is more prevalent than transnational trafficking".[8] One report from UNICEF gives the example of Tanzania, where "most girls in prostitution found in major cities were [internally] trafficked from rural regions."[9] Indeed the indications are that internal trafficking, within the confines of a country, is considerably larger than international trafficking.[10]

A misconception concerning the nature of human trafficking is that it involves transportation. One OSCE report advises:

The essential element in the Trafficking Protocol *is an action taken for the purpose of exploitation. Trafficking does not require transportation.*[11]

The *Trafficking in Persons Report 2008* notes that neither the *Palermo Protocol,* nor the United States' own federal legislation:

> ... *requires the movement of the victim. Movement is not necessary, as any person who is recruited, harbored, provided, or obtained through force, fraud, or coercion for the purpose of subjecting that person to involuntary servitude, forced labor, or commercial sex qualifies as a trafficking victim.*[12]

There are two other noteworthy elements to the *Palermo Protocol.* The protocol addresses the issue of consent and states that consent becomes "irrelevant where any of the means ... [listed in the definition] ... have been used".[13] This element of the protocol recognises "that core human rights cannot be waived".[14]

The issue of children, which the protocol defines as "any person under 18 years of age", and their exploitation is also addressed.[15] The United Nations definition shortened the previously given definition so that, where children are concerned, the means of trafficking become irrelevant. The definition of human trafficking as it applies to children is:

> *The recruitment, transportation, transfer, harbouring or receipt of a child for the purpose of exploitation shall be considered 'trafficking in persons' even if this does not involve any of the means set forth.*[16]

The issues of consent and means have a complex relationship. Where children are involved, the means and indeed consent become entirely immaterial. Where adults are concerned, the fact, for example, that a person consents to engage in the sex industry is irrelevant under the *Palermo Protocol* where they have been deceived about the exploitative conditions of the work or if they are subsequently forced to work in such conditions. Although beyond the scope of this work, this raises the interesting question of what constitutes non-exploitative conditions and has particular significance for the relationship between trafficking and prostitution.

Definition is then important. However, having provided a definition, the reader should be aware that it can limit our understanding of the complexities of human trafficking. Dr. Dina Siegel, Professor of Criminology at the Willem Pompe Institute of Utrecht University warns against "a 'black and white' picture, which is often reduced to a 'victims-offenders' presentation", while at the same time recognising it "would be wrong, on the other hand, to claim that all sex workers (legal and illegal) are working voluntarily".[17] As Dr. Siegel points out, there are two perils. Firstly, there is the peril of lowering the bar so low that every sex worker immediately becomes a victim. Here the concept becomes so generalised that those who have been deceived or coerced into a life of "modern-day slavery" become indistinguishable from those who have not.[18] Consequently, not only does a loose definition fail to identify the exploited but it leaves claims of their victimisation open to misguided criticisms such as being nothing more than "really concerned with patrolling sexual behaviour, and protecting stereotypical spiritual women from stereotypical animalistic men."[19] Secondly, there is the peril of raising the bar so high that almost nobody can meet the requirements of the definition. This is a real consideration. In the United States, the governing legislation is the *Victims of Trafficking and Violence Protection Act of 2000* (sometimes referred to as the *Trafficking Victims Protection Act of 2000* (TVPA)). This legislation recognises only "severe forms of trafficking", stating:

> *Victims of severe forms of trafficking should not be inappropriately incarcerated, fined, or otherwise penalized solely for unlawful acts committed as a direct result of being trafficked, such as using false documents, entering the country without documentation, or working without documentation.*[20]

Many questions remain about the adequacy of definition provided by the *Palermo Protocol*. No doubt, the debate will continue. Whatever emerges in the future, it is important that the focus should always remain on identifying victims of exploitation and ending their suffering.

[1]   United Nations Office on Drugs and Crime, n.d.

[2]   *Ibid.*

[3]   United Nations Office on Drugs and Crime., 2004, p. iii.

[4]   *Ibid.*, p. 42.

[5]   International Labour Organization (ILO), 2005, p. 9.

[6]   United Nations Children's Fund (UNICEF) Innocenti Research Centre, 2004, p. 14; International Organization for Migration (IOM), n.d; UNESCO, 2006, p. 11.

[7]   United States Department of State, 2011, p. 188.

[8]   *Ibid.*, p. 313.

[9]   United Nations Children's Fund (UNICEF) Innocenti Research Centre, 2004, p. 14.

[10] Lee, 2007, p. 60.

[11] Aronowitz *et al.*, 2010, p. 17.

[12] United States Department of State, 2008, p. 19.

[13] United Nations Office on Drugs and Crime, 2004, p. 43.

[14] United States Department of State, 2011, p. 37.

[15] United Nations Office on Drugs and Crime, 2004, p. 43.

[16] *Ibid.*, p. 43.

[17] Siegel, 2009, p. 9.

[18] Kim and Hreshchyshyn, 2005, p. 5.

[19] King, 2011.

[20] *Victims of Trafficking and Violence Protection Act, 2000*, Sec.102 (b)(19).

CHAPTER 9
THE FACE OF MODERN-DAY SLAVERY

The very mention of human trafficking may be enough to conjure mental images of victims exploited for sex in general and forced commercial sexual exploitation in particular. However, as the *Palermo Protocol* indicates, other forms of exploitation are possible. The trafficking of persons for the purpose of forced labour or removal of their organs are two such possibilities.

In 1930, the International Labour Organization (ILO), a specialist agency of the United Nations, defined forced labour as:

> ... *all work or service which is exacted from any person under the menace of any penalty and for which the said person has not offered himself voluntarily.*[1]

There are some exceptions to this definition, including those works undertaken for military service, for 'normal civic obligations', work undertaken in times of calamity or that undertaken as a result of a court conviction.[2] Human trafficking is one of the strategies used to feed the supply of workers into conditions of forced labour. In sub-Saharan Africa, 80% of the exploitation associated with human trafficking has nothing to do with sexual exploitation at all.[3]

One of the practices around the world closely associated with forced labour is that of debt bondage. The practice sometimes is known also as bonded or indentured labour. While the practice has been forbidden under international law, it continues to exist today.[4] The situation is very easily accomplished. A person in dire financial need accepts money from a future employer on the basis that it will be repaid through their work. Repaying the money is often impossible. Since the debt never goes away, neither does the obligation to work. The person is now in a situation where they are effectively a slave. Debt bondage is the "principal form of slavery in India, Nepal and Pakistan".[5] In some countries, the debt is passed from one generation of a family to the next. Thus it becomes possible for a person to have inherited a debt from their parents and for them to pass the debt on to a third generation. The monies involved may well be trivial by Western standards but that is of little consequence to the slave who has no capacity to repay them. Once a person is in this situation, there are all sorts of jobs that may be given them.

Andrees and Belser recognise that "most forced labour occurs in low-technology, labor-intensive activities or industries such as domestic work, agriculture, construction, or prostitution".[6] They also observe why this is so and their conclusions point to vulnerability. Where the production is focused on high volume, the work usually requires workers of a low level of education. Such workers may be more easily exploited. Additionally, the ability to lower labour costs has a very significant impact on profit where the production is labour-intensive. For Andrees and Belser, this means "employers in labor-intensive sectors may be more tempted to exploit workers".[7] At times though, the motivation is less subtle and may be attributed to outright greed:

> *Claims that child labor in the rug industry exists because producers cannot afford to pay full wages are spurious. To the contrary – the typical carpet weaving business model produces more than sufficient profits to pay full and fair wages; however, greed drives exploiters to utilize bonded, forced and underage labor to maximize profits in full violation of the law.*[8]

When one considers the comparatively low-tech, high-volume nature of work in developing countries, the potential scale of the problem becomes apparent. It is small wonder then that the estimated number of victims of forced labour, bonded labour and forced prostitution worldwide is 12.3 million persons.[9] Aside from those specified above, other industries also have been noted for their association with human trafficking – for example, begging, carpet weaving, brick making, mining, etc. Sometimes, these are referred to as '3D' jobs, meaning "dirty, degrading and dangerous".[10] A fourth 'D' – deadly – may be added as there are instances where the death of the victim fulfils the objective of the trafficker.

While organ removal is associated predominantly with non-lethal transplants, other practices occur. One of these is the issue of human sacrifice. A well-known case in contemporary times, one raised earlier in this publication by Dr. DeWan, is that of a five year-old boy from Nigeria by the name of Ikpomwosa.[11] The child became better known by the name that had been given him by authorities during the time they were trying to learn his identity: Adam. The fact that his case is known as the 'Torso in the Thames' indicates the circumstances under which he was found. When Adam's body was pulled from the British river in September 2001, the body was "without its legs, arms and head and had been entirely drained of its blood".[12] It is small wonder then that journalist Ronke Phillips recalls how, when the details emerged, "even the most hardened reporters [were] visibly shaken by the horror of what the police" revealed.[13] The fate of Ikpomwosa, or Adam as he was known to so many, showed that human sacrifice is not yet a practice consigned to history. In India, adults and children occasionally are murdered in sacrificial rites.[14] Indonesia and Africa feature as places where such humans have been sacrificed.[15] The U.S. Department of State notes:

> In 2010, a Zambian court sentenced a Zambian man to 18 years' imprisonment for selling his 7-year-old daughter for the purpose of harvesting her organs for use in ritual practices in Tanzania.[16]

Where such practices occur, an association with human trafficking is reasonable. In Adam's case, it was noted that he had been trafficked from Nigeria to the UK and it was likely his traffickers were aware that his journey would end in his death.[17]

A general principle of trafficking is that falling victim to one form of exploitation does not exclude a person from being exploited by another form also. This is a very real possibility. In addition, one also may escape one form of human trafficking only to find oneself captive to it in another place. If this happens, a person is said to have been re-trafficked.[18] In preying upon the vulnerable, traffickers exploit that vulnerability but traffickers also intensify the vulnerability so that victims become even more vulnerable and more likely to experience trafficking again. The story of Idrees is offered as an example:

> *Today Idrees, 27, is a free man, after nearly 10 years in bondage at a brick-kiln near ... the eastern Pakistani border city of Lahore. He won his freedom by selling his left kidney. With the Rs 90,000 ($1,500) he got, he was able to pay off a debt of around Rs 60,000 ($1,000) he and his elderly parents owed to the kiln owner.*

> *... he is once more in debt, having borrowed Rs 5,000 ($840) from a cousin a few days ago. "It's a pity I can't sell my other kidney", he said only half jokingly, adding: "But at least we are free. Allah (God) will help us now". Idrees's own ill-health since the surgery prevents him finding work ...[19]*

Idrees was vulnerable. He was living the life of a slave. The person to whom he owed money was able to exploit his financial vulnerability to place him in a position of slavery. Organ traffickers were able to exploit his predicament further by offering him a way out of his initial predicament through the sale of a kidney. Tragically, with each experience of exploitation, Idrees was worse off than he had been before. At the end, he had neither possession of his health nor was he entirely independent.

The idea of millions of people working away in conditions of slavery seems plausible enough given what is relayed to us here in the West about the poverty of most of our fellow human beings. However, forced labour is not a practice confined to poor nations. Those poor so readily exploited in other countries, often by their fellow citizens, may be brought to the West so that the same exploitation can occur here. There is no reason why the exploitation that makes so much financial sense in India, Africa or other parts of the world, would not make as much sense here.

The ILO gives this account of the exploitation of people who were trafficked into Britain for the purpose of forced labour:

> *A gang imported east European workers for illegal factory work ... They [the workers] were originally promised work permits, but were given false passports en route. They then attempted to escape the gang's control, but were subjected to such serious threats that they were forced to continue. On arrival they were informed of their conditions. They would work seven days a week, to repay the cost of both their transport to the United Kingdom and their food and accommodation while in that country. Once the debts had been cleared, they would be required to work for at least one year, for either no pay or at best a few pounds of 'pocket money' per week. Salaries were paid into a gang member's bank account. The workers were watched carefully, moved from house to house, and kept in isolation. Any breach of conditions, including work absences as a result of sickness, was added to their debt or deducted from their pocket money. Control was maintained through beatings and threats of assault on workers and their families back home.*[20]

In 2008, the *Trafficking in Persons Report* published a claim that might have been of interest to Ireland though it seems to have gone largely unobserved.[21] This claim was repeated more emphatically the following year. The *Trafficking in Persons Report 2009* narrative dealing with Australia reported (emphasis added):

> *Some men and women from several Pacific islands, India, the PRC, South Korea, the Philippines, **and Ireland** are fraudulently recruited to work temporarily in Australia, but subsequently are subjected to conditions of forced labor, including confiscation of travel documents, confinement, and threats of serious harm.*[22]

In 2008, the Federal Magistrates' Court in Perth imposed a substantial fine on a Australian company for exploiting migrant workers.[23] This is the probable basis for the claim made in the previous excerpt. Some of those exploited were Irish workers. All of them were on a special work permit that tied their stay in the country to their original employer. They were not entitled to move between employers and they were presented with undated work agreements while being denied the required documents outlining their rights. In practices tantamount to conditions of forced labour, they were threatened with summary deportation if they did not sign the document presented. The fine of AUD$174,000 was purported to be the largest such fine ever imposed under Australia's *Workplace Relations Act* and serves to illustrate the seriousness the court attached to the case.[24] The Magistrate, Toni Lucev, said of the violations that they were "deliberate and exploited vulnerable workers".[25] Senator Chris Evans, then Australian Minister for Immigration and Citizenship, recognised how unscrupulous employers might choose to exploit migrant workers, even in a booming economy.[26]

Clearly, the issue here was not sexual exploitation and yet many of the control measures one might have expected to see in an account of sexual exploitation are evident and can be afforded the same significance. This case serves several purposes. In the first instance, it serves to illustrate that violations of human dignity that occur in one part of the world are likely to occur in another. In the second instance, it demonstrates that the modern-day slavery imposed by traffickers upon workers indeed does occur in the Western world. Finally, the account illustrates how the methods employed by the traffickers remained the same even though the nature of the exploitation was different.

The issues discussed here are complex. Over the course of the past chapters, an exploration of how human trafficking might be defined has commenced. This exploration has focused initially on sexual exploitation to appreciate the link between power and process. Thereafter, it has continued to stretch the bounds of our understanding to include practices of forced labour, organ transplantation and other abuses committed against the dignity of the person. It becomes possible to understand trafficking in more general terms as a practice, not necessarily linked to a specific exploitation, by which an exploiter exploits the vulnerability of another to achieve whatever goal he or she may be pursuing. The true essence of trafficking becomes evident. Trafficking is not specifically about sexual exploitation or forced labour or organ transplantation or any other abuse. Yes, trafficking includes all of these things but, more centrally, it is about enslaving a human being to fulfil the selfish desires of another. If the reader accepts this as so, then the many faces of trafficking fall away to reveal it as a universal practice and this is why it is referred to, however it manifests itself, as "modern-day slavery".[27]

---

[1]   International Labour Organization (ILO), 1930, Article 2.1.

[2]   *Ibid.*, Article 2.2.

[3]   International Labour Organization, 2005, p. 13.

[4]   United Nations, 1957.

[5]   Upadhyaya and Anti-Slavery International, 2008, p. 5.

[6]   Andrees and Belser, 2009, p. 2.

[7]   *Ibid.*, p. 2.

[8]   Kara, 2011.

[9]   United States Department of State, 2010, p. 7; International Labour Organization, 2005, p. 12.

[10]   Amnesty International, 2005.

[11]   Phillips, 2011.

[12]   *Ibid.*

[13]   *Ibid.*

[14]   Bhaumik, 2010; McDougall, 2006; *The Times of India*, 2009.

[15]   Xinhuanet.com, 2006; Associated Press, 2008; AFP, 2005; United Nations Committee on the Elimination of Discrimination Against Women, 2010, p. 13; BBC News (UK), 2005.

[16]   United States Department of State, 2011, p. 390.

[17]   Phillips, 2011.

[18]   Kelleher *et al.*, 2009, p. 30; Goodey, 2004, p. 38.

[19] Integrated Regional Information Networks (IRIN), 2005.

[20] International Labour Organization, 2005, p. 54.

[21] United States Department of State, 2008, p. 61.

[22] United States Department of State, 2009, p. 67. Emphasis added.

[23] Bowen, 2008; GMANews.tv, 2008.

[24] GMANews.tv, 2008.

[25] *Ibid.*

[26] Bowen, 2008.

[27] Kim and Hreshchyshyn, 2005, p. 5; European Institute for Crime Prevention and Control affiliated with the United Nations (HEUNI), 2011, p. 11; Department of Justice, Equality & Law Reform, n.d., p. 4.

CHAPTER 10
CASE STUDY 2:
THOMAS CARROLL

In 2008, as the global recession continued to deepen, things took a turn for the worse for Carlow-born Thomas Carroll's family-run business. Amongst the employees were his South African wife, Shamiela Clark, and his daughter, Toma. Operating from a former vicarage in the Welsh hamlet of Castlemartin, the business had been thriving, returning up to €1 million in profits annually.[1] Mr. Carroll's problems were not linked to the prevailing financial gloom but rather to the fact that his empire of brothels, situated in Irish towns and cities such as Athlone, Belfast, Cavan, Carlow, Drogheda, Enniscorthy, Kilkenny, Lurgan, Mullingar, Newbridge, Newry, Omagh and Sligo, had become a matter of interest to a specialist unit of An Garda Síochána, the Irish national police service. The Garda's Organised Crime Unit had issued a European arrest warrant and, in December 2008, the Welsh police arrested Thomas Carroll.[2]

What soon became apparent was the level of success Mr. Carroll had enjoyed. His organisation was described as "the biggest vice ring in the country's history".[3] Some of the success may be attributable to cheap labour, for it was noted that trafficked girls were present and of these "some [were] as young as 15" years of age.[4] Through their services, Carroll was reportedly getting a return of €160 for every half-hour they worked.[5] There are indications that it may have been possible to charge substantially more than this rate at times. Indeed, it was reported that "one girl alone made €6,800 over three days in an Athlone brothel".[6] This contrasts sharply against the humble origins of the women and girls, though they saw little of the money they earned for him. Often their pay was not money at all, but rather "food and condoms".[7]

The women who worked in the brothels came from all over the world. Some had come from South America and Africa, while others had come from eastern Europe.[8] Some had worked in prostitution previously. Among those discovered were some who had been trafficked and six of whom were girls and women from Nigeria.[9] In most cases, the victims of trafficking are so overwhelmed by fear of their traffickers that they are unwilling to help police. In this instance, the police found the two young Nigerian girls were willing to help.[10] Statements given to the police claimed that they "were tricked into working in the sex industry".[11]

All of these Nigerians had come from "poor family backgrounds, having lost one or both parents".[12] One of the girls revealed that they had been attempting to flee her sexually-abusive father. She reported that the abuse had started when she was just eight years old and that she had had three abortions by the time she was 20. One day, she overheard her father talking on the phone, discussing sacrificing her to a cult. She decided to flee Nigeria and learned of a European woman whom she thought could help her.[13] It is likely that this woman was a trafficker. All of the girls and women had believed they were coming to Ireland "for a better life".[14] Evidence given in court showed that the young women "believed they were ... to enjoy an education or become hairdressers or seamstresses".[15] One of the girls was just 14 years of age when she was trafficked from Nigeria.[16]

Prior to their departure for Europe, the issue of money was discussed and, though their destination had not been finalised, the expense of travelling was raised. An understanding was reached that traffickers would make the necessary arrangements for travel, even covering the expense. Consequently, those travelling would soon be in a position where they were indebted to those offering them jobs. The girls and women would have to work upon arrival in order to refund the debt incurred. In order to be assured that these monies would be repaid in their entirety, it was deemed reasonable that those travelling would be bonded to their traffickers through Voodoo.[17]

The Voodoo rites endured seem particularly gruesome:

> One was forced to sleep in a coffin to "put the fear of death" in her. Menstrual blood was drawn into a padlock, locked, and thrown in the river to signify their lives were in the hands of the river goddess, said investigators.

> Live chickens were killed and the victims made to eat the raw hearts.

> Fingernail clippings and pubic hair cuttings were taken, and retained, to "instil the fear of God in them" and show they could be "metaphysically" reached wherever they were. Often the girls were naked, and one was cut all over her body with blades, said investigators.[18]

Within a few days of arriving in Ireland, the Nigerians were working as prostitutes and in "their own minds, they were tied by the oath of obedience" each had taken, ensuring their compliance.[19] The full implications of disobedience were understood as it had been explained to them by the:

> ... shaman or witch doctor back in their home country that they would die, or someone they loved would die, if they did not adhere to this code of obedience.[20]

The women and girls also recalled how Carroll "controlled them by beatings and rape" and, while he was not a witch doctor, he fully understood the potency of using "terrifying Voodoo threats to keep them from running away".[21] These were just some of the forms of abuse used against the victims.

One can scarcely imagine the horror of their predicament and their state of mind. However, even being upset was a problem for their captors and one girl endured verbal abuse as she was told that her bouts of crying were "putting the customers off".[22]

Victims were moved around regularly, not only for the purpose of providing "variety" to customers, but also for the purpose of disorienting the women and girls, likely facilitating social isolation and reducing the risk that they might escape.[23] Their isolation was made worse by the fact that they were not acquainted with anybody in Ireland and "having little or no English", there was little prospect of them forming any such acquaintances.[24] Indeed this may have been part of the appeal of using women trafficked from Africa.[25] Their situation was not helped by the fact that they "made no money because they were endlessly paying off money to Carroll" and if they "missed a client [appointment] they were required to pay the fee themselves".[26]

There were times when the abuse of the trafficked women failed to obtain the compliance required. Carroll and his associates were able to deal with this problem by contacting the trafficking gang that had originally sourced the women for him. When contact was made with these people in Africa and the situation explained, the traffickers took ownership of the problem. The gang would travel to the homes of the families of the victims where they would advise the families that their womenfolk were causing trouble in relation to the payment of their debt. Then the gang would proceed to assault the victim's family members. Occasionally, the victims then were called by telephone and their assaulted family member allowed speak to them so that the latter might berate them for the hardship their misbehaviour had brought upon their family.[27]

The sophistication of the operation was observed by several parties. Technology played a significant role. During the course of the raid in Wales, police "found 70 mobile phones, all linked to adverts placed on sexual services websties [sic] or in newspapers".[28] Journalist Jim Cusack elaborates:

> Carroll advertised his prostitutes on the "Escorts Ireland" website ... The whole operation depended on the use of mobile phone numbers, some of which have been in operation for more than a decade.[29]

The *Carlow People* newspaper described the sophistication of the operation as allowing the Welsh base to operate as a form of headquarters, co-ordinating operations and making arrangements important for the day-to-day running of the business. Adverts were placed detailing the services available and providing contact information. Arrangements were made to ensure there was always an adequate supply of accommodation. Incoming calls were processed and bookings made. The women were informed of their schedule, the rates they were to charge punters and any rules that they were to abide by. With all of the information to hand, it was easy for Carroll to keep track of the monies being received by all of the women, thus ensuring that nothing was kept back from him.[30] His wife did much of the telephone work, co-ordinating as many as 300 calls each day from clients.[31] Conor Lally observes:

> Their 'business model' demonstrated how the Internet and mobile phones allowed them to run a business in 18 towns across rural Ireland.[32]

Particular aspects seem to be critical to these kinds of operations. Carroll spent Stg£28,580 on newspaper advertising in one year alone; one mobile phone bill came to Stg£5,2000 in just three months and ran to 5,000 pages.[33] Small wonder then Jim Cusack reports:

> Gardaí say operations like Carroll's could be closed down here in a single day if Garda management was to forcefully request that mobile phone companies close down the mobile phone numbers advertised on the websites. A recommendation to this effect was made by a detective superintendent four years ago but received no response.[34]

One of the draft adverts discovered by the Serious Organised Crime Unit (SOCA), which raided Carroll's Welsh premises, read:

> African Nandi, very petite tanned chocolate delight, petite slim size 8, 34C but leggy flexible kinky.[35]

What the advert did not mention of course was that 'African Nandi' was trafficked, that she was engaging in prostitution under duress and punters availing of the services advertised consequently were engaging in an act of rape.

Frustratingly, "charges of trafficking against the couple [Thomas Carroll and Shamiela Clark] were not pursued after they agreed to plead guilty to charges of controlling prostitution and money laundering, in February 2010".[36] Thomas Carroll is presently "serving a seven-year term for vice and money laundering offences".[37] In March 2011, he was served with a confiscation order by Cardiff Crown Court. The order, made under the *Proceeds of Crime Act*, demanded €2.2 million from him.[38]

One of the aspects of cases such as Carroll's is the unwillingness to remain within the confines of what would otherwise be termed prostitution. As already outlined, his empire of vice had surpassed any other in Ireland. His call centre was receiving hundreds of calls per day and, each time the phone rang, his operation was receiving at least €160. The extent of his wealth was such that the British Crown believed him capable of paying a confiscation order in the millions. Yet this was not enough; much more profit could be extracted. By engaging in human trafficking, Carroll was able to increase the profitability of his operation. The real cost was the immeasurable suffering imposed upon his victims, which included rape. Some of those who suffered were children.

---

1   Lally, 2010b.
2   *Ibid.*
3   O'Clery, 2010.
4   BBC News (UK), 2010.
5   Davies, 2010.
6   *Sunday World*, 2010.
7   *Ibid.*
8   BBC News (UK), 2010; Lally, 2010b.
9   Davies, 2010.
10 O'Clery, 2010.
11 *Sunday World*, 2010.
12 Davies, 2010.

13 Lally, 2010a.
14 *Irish Examiner*, 2011.
15 BBC News (UK), 2011a.
16 Davies, 2010.
17 Lally, 2010b.
18 Davies, 2010.
19 Reilly, 2010.
20 *Ibid.*
21 *Sunday World*, 2010.
22 Reilly, 2010.
23 Lally, 2010b.
24 Lally, 2010c.
25 Lally, 2010a.
26 *Carlow People*, 2010.
27 Lally, 2010b.
28 Davies, 2010.
29 Cusack, 2010a.
30 *Carlow People*, 2010.
31 BBC News (UK), 2011a.
32 Lally, 2010c.
33 Davies, 2010.
34 Cusack, 2010a.
35 Davies, 2010.
36 BBC News (UK), 2010.
37 BBC News (UK), 2011a.
38 RTÉ News (Ireland), 2011b.

CHAPTER 11
THE ORIGINS AND IMPLICATIONS OF TRAFFICKING

Trafficking almost always can be associated with personal and national tragedy. Calamities produce vulnerability and it is this vulnerability that traffickers exploit. The largest such tragedy affecting most people on the face of the planet today is that of poverty. It should be of no surprise that poverty is very often identified as the issue that propels people to escape their predicament, an act that leads to their enslavement by traffickers.[1] Accounts of victimisation, given on television, in newspapers and on the Internet, so often start with the words that the victim had been seeking nothing more than "a better life".[2]

Of course, there are other personal crises that exacerbate the effects of poverty and make people even more likely to seek out a better life. For example, the breakdown of marriage, the wish to escape from an abusive relationship or the loss of a spouse are recognised factors that increase vulnerability and especially so in the case of women. The breakup of a marriage is one such crisis and it tends to have profoundly more consequences for women than for their former spouse.[3] Bereavement too has profound implications for those left behind, especially if they had been dependent on the deceased for their means of survival. In parts of the world where the scourge of HIV/AIDS infects so many and kills without pause, bereavement is obviously a commonplace consequence and so too the vulnerability that accompanies it.

Problems concerning national crises are recognised contributors to the spread of trafficking. Famine and earthquakes are two national crises capable of contributing to the trafficking of persons.[4] Violence, armed conflict and all-out war are other forms of national crisis and peoples flee them *en masse*. All are recognised contributors to the vulnerability exploited by traffickers.[5] Of course, sometimes political unrest or the rule of tyrannical regimes can propagate the personal crises that compel persons to flee. In testimony given before the United States House Foreign Affairs Subcommittee on Terrorism, Nonproliferation, and Trade, Holly Burkhalter, the U.S. Policy Director of Physicians for Human Rights, observed:

> *It is a cruel irony that many ... women and girls who are trafficked into brothels ... were fleeing a regime where rape and sexual violence are systemic.*[6]

Economic decline or the failure of an economy to develop is another such national crisis that drives people into conditions of poverty and vulnerability.[7]

Deception plays an important role in trafficking as previously described. The circumstances under which trafficking emerges themselves can be deceiving. Trafficking may occur under conditions of great national hope. Political change, even seemingly positive changes, can be accompanied by profoundly negative consequences. One such immense change that occurred only 20 years ago was the demise of the Soviet Union. The event was welcomed by people on both sides of the Iron Curtain and automatically one would tend to conclude that the event assured greater freedom, especially for those who lived under communism. Unfortunately, life is never quite so simple and even political and economic progress brings with it negative consequences. According to Lee:

> *The collapse of the Soviet communist regimes and the subsequent incorporation of Eastern Europe into global capitalism, and a more recent eastward enlargement of the EU, have arguably turned this region [of Eastern Europe] into "a perfect hub for international human trafficking".*[8]

The practices of modernity are another problem. The advances made through globalisation have come at great expense to developing nations. Siddarth Kara conducted "over 150 interviews with sex trafficking victims in brothels and shelters" across the globe.[9] Kara observes, as others have, the impact of globalisation on the peoples of third world countries and the consequences for human trafficking. He writes:

> *Sex trafficking is one of the ugliest contemporary actualizations of global capitalism because it was directly produced by the harmful inequalities spread by the process of economic globalization: deepening of rural poverty, increased economic disenfranchisement of the poor, the net extraction of wealth and resources from poor economies into richer ones, and the broad-based erosion of real human freedoms across the developing world.[10]*

Whatever the cause leading to the vulnerability, there is adequate evidence to show that women tend to be the ones most adversely affected.[11] Conscious of the vulnerability presented by women and children in the face of these circumstances, one study reasons:

> *... patterns of instability, oppression and discrimination may place women and children at greater risk, with social and cultural prejudices and the prevalence of gender violence presenting additional challenges to their effective protection from trafficking.[12]*

Greater meaning is obtained by looking at particular cases, focusing on particular countries. There is peril though in selecting one country for such scrutiny. To suppose, or indeed to be led to believe, that the problems of humanity are vested in any one place, one people or any one time would be to ignore the harshest lessons of history. Whether it is from Baltimore to Barbary, or from 1631 to contemporary times, the practice of slavery remains constant. The seemingly endless pages of contemporary reports on human trafficking are enough to attest to its presence amongst, victimisation of, and practice by, peoples across the globe. Examination of specific cases is useful nonetheless. Considerable focus has been given to Ireland, the United Kingdom, the United Arab Emirates, India, Indonesia and Australia in exploring how persons are exploited. It is to Nigeria that the exploration now turns to understand how it is that persons come to be exploited.

THE EXPLOITATION OF VULNERABILIY

The U.S. Central Intelligence Agency's *World Factbook* describes Nigeria as comprising 155 million people.[13] A few figures stand out in revealing some of the hardships experienced in the country, hardships that amount to personal tragedy. With deaths numbering 91.54 per 1,000, the country has one of the highest infant mortality rates in the world. At birth, one can expect to live a total of 47.5 years. HIV/AIDS infections total 3.3 million persons, placing the country third globally in this regard, with an estimated 220,000 people dying each year from the infection.[14] National crises are present too. For nearly 16 years, the country had been under continuous military rule. All of this changed in 1999 when democracy was restored but the country continues to be besieged by political, economic and social problems.[15]

Even from a cursory glance of the realities on the ground in Nigeria, it is appreciable why the country features so prominently in reports on trafficking. If hardship results in vulnerability and vulnerability results in trafficking, then Nigeria ought to be a significant country for the supply of victims and so it is. In Holland, the National Rapporteur on Trafficking in Human Beings reported that Nigerians were the only nationality to "appear in the top five in each of the 10 years reported".[16] Fifty Nigerian women are known to have been subjected to human trafficking in Sweden in 2009.[17] In Ireland, figures published by Ruhama revealed that, of the 80 trafficked women supported by the charity in 2010, the majority, 61%, were Nigerian.[18] Of the 2,000 women trafficked into Italy each year, it is reported that 60% are from Nigeria.[19]

Poignantly, even in Palermo, where one of the cornerstone international agreements aimed at combating human trafficking was agreed, "trafficked Nigerian women have become synonymous with prostitution".[20]

Each country brings with it problems specific to its own predicament. The breakup of marriage was identified earlier as a factor contributing to vulnerability and thereafter to trafficking. Traditionally, Nigerian parents would care for their children irrespective of the status of their marriage. This has changed in recent years and now "many abandon their children when the marriage ends in separation".[21] Sr. Monica Onwunali of The Congregation of Sisters of Our Lady of Apostles (OLA) works in Rome with Unione Superiore Maggiori d'Italia (USMI) to combat human trafficking. She has experience of the issue in Italy and in her native Nigeria. Sr. Onwunali acknowledges the problem of family breakdown as a factor contributing to human trafficking in Nigeria.[22] "A woman will have five or six children and abandon them to have children with another man ... [thus the combination of] big families and broken homes" contributes to vulnerability in Nigerian society, she says. Children then are "left to grow by themselves ... when there is no education, no family background". In this way, recruiters or traffickers who seem to have the answers to these children's aspirations must seem like a blessing; "the light becomes the trafficker".

The role of HIV/AIDS also has been identified as a factor contributing to trafficking. By 2003, 10% of all the children in Nigeria between the ages of 0 and 17 years of age, a total of 7 million children, were orphans.[23] Just over one-quarter (26%) of these, or 1.82 million, had lost one or both of their parents to the infection.[24] The implications of this situation from a child-protection perspective are clear.

EXPLOITATION BY WITCHCRAFT

Another issue encountered in Nigeria is that of witchcraft. The practice of Juju is a cultural phenomenon in some parts of Nigeria, as affirmed earlier by Dr. DeWan. One report notes:

> *Oaths of secrecy are administered to the soon-to-be-trafficked persons and their families at the point of recruitment ... especially in Edo and Delta States.*[25]

Sr. Onwunali explains that Juju has not always been a negative element of Nigerian society: "it is only now that Juju has become negative" through the exploitation of traffickers.[26] Sr. Onwunali recounts that Juju was the traditional African court system. Every town had its own shrine. If a person stole or did something that was deemed wrong, they could be taken to the shrine to swear an oath to affirm their innocence. In taking the oath, the person would understand the serious consequences of lying, including death. Additionally, those taking oaths appreciated that, in lying under oath, one also could bring hardship upon one's own people.

Sr. Onwunali sees how human traffickers have taken something that was important to African society and twisted it. "Juju used to be something positive for the people", allowing some measure of justice in society, she states. Juju is now a mechanism to ensure that traffickers can instil fear into those whom they wish to control and that they will be assured of a return on the money invested in the trafficking of a person. According to Sr. Onwunali, traffickers have "turned Juju into [a] shrine of evil".

She explains that these shrines are not buildings *per se*. Shrines can be somewhat akin to the historical Irish tradition of the mass rock. The shrine is usually associated with a place of some geographical importance such as one marked by a rock. Other geographical features, especially those near water, also bear some significance.

An important part of the ritual is the making of the spell and this is full of symbolism. The person who concocts the spell is referred to as a "Juju doctor" or a "Juju priest". In describing the process, Sr. Onwunali details how body parts, such as hair and nail clippings, are taken from the body, to be used in concoctions or spells that form part of the oath. In effect, "they have sacrificed you to the spirits if you don't fulfil your oaths". The real reason for the oaths, as Sr. Onwunali is all too keenly aware, is that it stops the victims from fleeing: "So that you will not run away, that's why they seal the arrangement with the oaths. ... The African traditional belief is that oaths must be fulfilled". She recalls how she has often heard African prostitutes in Italy, who have entered the work through human trafficking, say, "Sister, what can I do ... you want me ... to bring calamity to my people". She is keenly aware that the traffickers have not invested, as they claim, very significant monies to transport their victims to Europe and she advises victims "Nobody has spent more than €5,000" to bring them to Europe, let alone the exorbitant figures the traffickers often claim.

Witchcraft plays a multi-faceted role. In some cases, those who take the oaths ascribe a benefit to the rites. Traffickers are only too happy to employ the services of Juju doctors, as in addition to the rites binding the victim to the trafficker they also compel the victim to keep secret the trafficker's role. A report from UNESCO provides a fuller explanation:

> These traditional oaths involve the use of body parts of the trafficked persons, such as blood, fingernails, and hair from the genitalia or the head. Traditional priests prepare ceremonial drinks in their shrines that are taken by the future trafficked persons and their relatives.

> This traditional oath-taking is designed to instil fear, promising death, madness or terrible harm in the event that the trafficked persons reveal the trafficker's secrets. ... the trafficked girls are made to repeat several times, "If I don't pay I will go crazy or I will be killed".

> The concoctions taken during the oath are also believed to help attract sex customers while protecting the trafficked persons from

contracting HIV, or to prevent detection by immigration authorities.

Some returnees cited the taking of these ceremonial drinks as a reason for their having the confidence to go [to Europe and elsewhere] in the first place, thereby illustrating their psychological potency; believing in their efficacy they will neither claim to be trafficked nor reveal the identity of their traffickers.[27]

While many people are trafficked abroad UNESCO has observed that over the past 20 years the practice of trafficking women and children within the borders of Nigeria has grown. People from rural communities are trafficked to the big cities.[28]

FURTHER EFFECTS

Looking at external trafficking, much of the attention placed upon Nigeria as a source country may be the outcome of the comparatively high attention the country receives in reported cases of human trafficking in Europe. However, Europe is only one of the destinations to which Nigerians are trafficked. In 2010, senior officials of the Nigerian government's anti-trafficking agency, NAPTIP, visited Mali on foot of "reports that 20,000 to 40,000 Nigerians were being held there in forced prostitution".[29]

The *Trafficking Persons Report 2011* describes Nigeria as:

... a source, transit, and destination country for women and children subjected to forced labor and sex trafficking. Trafficked Nigerian women and children are recruited from rural, and to a lesser extent urban, areas within the country's borders – women and girls for domestic servitude and sex trafficking, and boys for forced labor in street vending, domestic servitude, mining, stone quarries, agriculture, and begging. Nigerian women and children are taken from Nigeria to other West and Central African countries, including Gabon, Cameroon, Ghana, Chad, Benin, Togo, Niger, Burkina Faso, the Central African Republic, and The Gambia, as well as South Africa, for the same purposes.[30]

Aside from the heavy price paid by individuals who are exploited, another such price is paid by the states like Nigeria. States already impoverished by political, economic and social upheaval consequentially experience an "irretrievable depletion of human capital".[31] The impact of mass emigration on a society is well-understood but trafficking adds another dynamic to this social phenomenon. Thousands upon thousands of people leave their communities and their countries. These are sometimes *the best and the brightest*, the most mobile. This was exemplified in one study which revealed that, in Nigeria, it was not "the poorest ones but those" who were slightly more affluent that ended up being trafficked.[32] Countries like Nigeria find that, having invested so much of what they can ill-afford on their youth, the state cannot get a return on that investment. Consequently, core state services such as education and healthcare, decline. The economy suffers in a number of ways. The decline of education and the depletion of human capital leaves the national "labour force ill-equipped to compete in a global economy where success is based on skilled workers".[33]

Having endured so much exploitation, resulting in so much misery, by so many different means, one might expect that a seemingly once inexhaustible list of exploitation was now spent. This is not the case and UNESCO notes there is one final parting gift bestowed upon those victimised and their states of origin. In a final act of cruel fate, the human capital, of which the state was depleted, now returns home, itself depleted save by the addition of HIV/AIDS. With nowhere else to turn, perhaps having been disposed of by their exploiters, or deported by the authorities of the country where their exploitation occurred, they return home.

The very presence of infections, such as HIV/AIDS, in a state creates potential for conditions of vulnerability. The full potential of the vulnerability is achieved in states where the prevailing political, economic and social conditions are already in chaos. The resultant vulnerability then is exploited by traffickers. "Simultaneously, trafficking increases the number of HIV infections".[34] This has two immediately identifiable consequences. The first of these consequences is that escalating rates of infection sap limited highly-valued healthcare and monetary resources in an already-struggling state. The second of these consequences is that trafficking further contributes to the prevalence of infection in society, a significant source of vulnerability. Predictably, more people suffer, more die and the numbers infected increase much faster than if trafficking had not been present in the state. Those left behind are immediately vulnerable to exploitation by traffickers. In these ways, human trafficking not only undermines the right of a people to a state, it denies that right entirely.

1   Haynes, 2004, p. 226; Poudel and Carryer, 2000, p. 74; Miller, 2008, p. 54; Kelleher *et al.*, 2009, p. 1; Nic Gabhan, 2006, p. 529; Cole, 2006, p. 217.
2   *Irish Examiner*, 2011; Viuhko & Jokinen, 2009, p. 13; Buckley, 2004, p. 30; *Al Jazeera*, 2011.
3   Miller, 2008, p. 52; United Nations Children's Fund (UNICEF) Innocenti Research Centre, 2004, p. 6; United States Department of State, 2010, p. 34.
4   Gammelli, 2011; Buckley, 2004, p. 30.
5   UNESCO, 2006, p. 14; International Labour Organization, 2005, p. 51; Elabor-Idemudia, 2003, p. 104.
6   Burkhalter, 2004.
7   International Labour Organization, 2005, p. 51; Joon and Fu, 2008, p. 513.
8   Lee, 2007, p. 15.
9   Kara, 2009, preface.
10   *Ibid.*, p. 4.
11   Kim and Hreshchyshyn, 2005, p. 6; Kelleher *et al.*, 2009, p. 35.
12   United Nations Children's Fund (UNICEF) Innocenti Research Centre, 2004, p. 5.
13   Central Intelligence Agency (CIA), 2011.
14   *Ibid.*
15   *Ibid.*
16   National Rapporteur on Trafficking in Human Beings, 2010, p. 94.
17   Polisen, 2010, p. 12.

18 Ruhama, 2011, p. 10.

19 Joon and Fu, 2008, p. 497.

20 Cole, 2006, p. 217.

21 UNESCO, 2006, p. 37.

22 Interview given September 2011.

23 UNESCO, 2006, p. 37.

24 *Ibid.*, p. 39.

25 *Ibid.*, p. 36.

26 Interview given September 2011.

27 UNESCO, 2006, p. 36.

28 *Ibid.*, p. 22.

29 United States Department of State, 2011, p. 279.

30 *Ibid.*, p. 279.

31 UNESCO, 2006, p. 61.

32 Miller, 2008, p. 55.

33 UNESCO, 2006, p. 61.

34 *Ibid.*, p. 39.

CHAPTER 12

PROSTITUTION, TRAFFICKING AND MONEY

In 2003, then U.S. President George W. Bush issued *National Security Presidential Directive 22: Trafficking in Persons*, declaring:

> *Prostitution and related activities, which are inherently harmful and dehumanizing, contribute to the phenomenon of trafficking in persons.*[1]

The directive made by President Bush attributed the existence of prostitution as sufficient to contribute to trafficking in persons. Over time the U.S. State Department issued even more robust claims, especially in relation to the issue of legalisation or even the tolerance of prostitution. The State Department claimed that prostitution provides "a facade behind which traffickers for sexual exploitation operate."[2] In response to the assertion that prostitution promotes trafficking, the anthropologist and filmmaker David Feingold responded:

> *According to the State Department Web site, "Where prostitution is legalized or tolerated, there is a greater demand for human trafficking victims and nearly always an increase in the number of women and children trafficked into commercial sex slavery". By this logic, the state of Nevada [where prostitution is legal in designated places] should be awash in foreign sex slaves.*[3]

Some years after President Bush issued his 2003 Presidential Directive linking prostitution to trafficking and after Feingold offered his rebuttal, Jill Morris of the Not For Sale Campaign testified before the Nevada State Legislature:

Because of its legal brothel industry, Nevada is a haven for sex traffickers who force young girls and boys into prostitution.[4]

Claims as to facts are always helpful but explanations for those facts invariably prove more valuable. The question arises then as to why prostitution would lead to human trafficking. There are doubtlessly many perspectives that could be adopted to analyse the argument. One possibility involves a fairly straightforward application of economics. The economic model asks merely that one presumes and accepts that all participants in the scenario in question are acting so as to maximise their financial reward.[5] One can dispense with moral judgements. Indeed in an economic approach, there is no room for morality. Decisions are made solely on the basis of a "calculation of costs and benefits". [6] The costs may be monetary but they may also go beyond this and may include legal sanction if the actor is apprehended while acting illegally. The benefits most certainly will be monetary. In summary, this perspective presumes that people will act in their own best interest to maximise rewards while at the same time being conscious of the risks. The only factor that needs to be ascertained is the balance of risks and rewards. If the rewards are sufficiently high and the risks sufficiently low, then rationality alone ought to attest to what will happen and what is happening.

The first step involves applying the economic model to prostitution in Ireland and it is with the financial rewards that the exploration commences. Estimates provided by Ruhama reported that, in Ireland, on "any day up to 1,000 women and girls are available for purchase for sex".[7] Irish national television broadcaster RTÉ concluded that there are "up to 700 women advertising sex for sale on escort agency websites" alone.[8] Demand then is significant. If there was no demand, there would be no supply. During the time Thomas Carroll was operating, he was charging punters €160 for every half-hour his women worked.[9] There are indications though that the recession has affected prostitution in Ireland. Rates on one site are advertised as €100 per half-hour and €200 per hour. This is lower than Thomas Carroll was reportedly getting some years ago. Present day figures of 1,000 women and girls working in prostitution illustrates that the demand continues to support the numbers engaged. Even after discounting, the rates charged are €200 per hour and the fact that prices remain stable demonstrates that the demand also continues to support this level of charging. Therefore, once can conclude that the rewards accrued through prostitution in Ireland remain high.

Having accounted for the rewards, the focus now turns to the issue of risk. Two risks are readily conceived. The first is the risk of punishment by legal sanction. Technically, prostitution itself is not illegal in Ireland but specific activities associated with prostitution in Ireland are illegal. Under Ireland's *Criminal Law (Sexual Offences) Act, 1993*, activities such as soliciting, directing or controlling the activities of a prostitute and maintaining a brothel are just some of those associated with prostitution that are prohibited by the law.[10] The second risk is associated with market deterioration but there is little reason to suppose there is any significant investment by brothel operators so there is little risk of loss since little has been invested.

In this instance, the balance of risk and reward is a foregone conclusion. The extent of prostitution in Ireland is evident, totalling as many as 1,000 prostitutes. Persons organising prostitution in Ireland have weighed up the risk and the reward: infringement of Ireland's *Criminal Law (Sexual Offences) Act, 1993* versus a share in revenues earned at a rate of €200 per hour for every prostitute working during that hour. Brothel operators continue to pursue prostitution because they balance the rationality of pursuing such high rewards against what they perceive to be low or acceptable risks. Thus the scales are tipped in favour of reward on the basis of a rational commitment to economics.

The second step is similar to the first, save that the economic model is now applied to human trafficking. The rewards are much as they were before. The victim of human trafficking forced into commercial sex slavery is still sold at usual market rates. The difference in this instance is that a greater share of the €200 earned from each hour's work, from each victim, is allocated to the brothel operator.

The focus now turns again to the issue of risk. Two risks are readily conceived. The first again is that of legal sanction. This is probably quite low. Until quite recently, no one in Ireland had ever "been convicted in the Irish courts for human trafficking or been given a significant sentence for aggravated pimping".[11] This changed in 2010 when the first two convictions were secured under Ireland's new *Criminal Law (Human Trafficking) Act, 2008*.[12] Overall, it is likely the case that operators of brothels have incurred no more legal sanction for trafficking than they would have for regular prostitution-related offences. The second risk is again associated with market deterioration. The risk here is the same as it was in the first step of the model, so no additional cost need be apportioned.

At this point, a judgement is needed as to the balance of risk and reward. Recall for a moment the rules of the economic approach. The approach is primarily about assessing the balance between *risk* and *reward*. As a decision rooted entirely in economics, it is one that requires no moral judgment whatsoever. The judgement is purely economic and presumes only that participants will act in accordance with their own economic self-interest. In the first instance, the economic approach illustrated how brothel operators had weighed up the risk and the reward: infringement of Ireland's *Criminal Law (Sexual Offences) Act, 1993* versus a share in revenues earned at a rate of €200 per hour for every prostitute working during that hour and had come down in favour of pursuing the rewards. In this second instance, the rewards are even greater, bestowing an even greater portion of the work of the sex worker upon the brothel operator. The risks are largely the same as they were in the first step of the approach. Thus economic rationality alone is sufficient to show why brothel operators would choose to pursue human trafficking, given that the risks are the same as prostitution and the rewards considerably greater than the activity in which they already engage. This is why Kara says:

Sex slavery is primarily a crime of economic benefit; that is, the slave owner exploits slaves to minimize labor costs and maximize profits.[13]

It is likely for this reason that:

The ILO does not draw hard and fast distinctions between trafficking for sexual exploitation on the one hand and for forced labour on the other. For the ILO, forced commercial sexual exploitation is one form of forced labour.[14]

The same approach can be applied globally, as the risks and rewards can be quantified with reasonable accuracy. Bearing in mind that it does not distinguish between forced commercial sexual exploitation and other forms of labour exploitation, the ILO states:

The total illicit profits produced in one year by trafficked forced labourers are estimated to be about US$32 billion ... Half of this profit is made in industrialized countries (US$15.5 billion) and close to one-third in Asia (US$9.7 billion). Globally, this represents an average of approximately US$13,000 per year for each forced labourer.[15]

So too can the risks be quantified globally. Figures provided by the United States government reveal that, in 2009, only 4,501 persons were successfully prosecuted across the world for human trafficking and forced labour offences. This is negligible compared to the estimated 12.3 million victims worldwide.[16] Thus the risks associated with human trafficking traditionally have been low: little risk to money and little risk of legal sanction. There is little reason to suppose that a person engaged in organising prostitution has taken on any additional risk by also engaging in human trafficking. The paradox is that, by looking at prostitution from the perspective of a brothel operator, the perspective is more likely to support the link between prostitution and human trafficking than to erode it. The rewards are so significant and the risks so low that making the extra return is a straightforward matter of rational behaviour and economics. In the words of Siddarth Kara, "Slave labor makes profits soar".[17]

Many of the characteristics exhibited by those who engage in prostitution reflect the priority of an economic perspective. For example, the recession is overtly acknowledged on one Irish website, with punters invited to "Ride out the Recession with budget female escorts".[18] The reference to "budget" is noteworthy and demonstrates four economic aspects. Firstly, as Andrees points out, that pimps and other actors, conscious of what is being sought by the punter, have "responded to changing pattern of demand".[19] One website allows punters to provide reviews of their experience and these reviews are publicly available. Some reflect the points being made here. They are reproduced *verbatim* with misspellings and other errors:

> *A little too expensive especially in a recession, thats the only reason i wouldn't return*[20]
>
> *there are still some charging €200/30mins, they do not know about recession yet!* [21]

The response in the form of lower prices recognises that punters cannot afford to pay high prices in times of recession. Secondly, this response reveals that operators in the prostitution business logically may be getting a lower return, assuming unit transactions remain steady, with incoming monies declining and with costs remaining relatively stagnant. So, as long as reducing prices has not increased business, those engaged in the sale of sexual services will be making less money. If the price changes provided here are reflected across the rest of prostitution in Ireland, then prices will have declined by 37.5%, hence there is less reward. This would certainly be a motivating factor to source cheaper labour through human trafficking. Thirdly, references to the recession could have been predicted by the application of an economic perspective. Fourthly, it confirms the suitability of an economic perspective in which brothel operators are acting rationally, in response to market conditions.

In an interview with Mary Crilly of Ireland's Sexual Violence Centre, she noted how prostitutes are treated by pimps as though they are nothing more than merchandise: "the pimps will talk about them as merchandise".[22] Interestingly this too attests to the application of economics. As far as the pimps are concerned, they are not dealing with people but rather with products. Even the very language used, which describes the victim in commoditised terms, informs the observer of the trafficker's perspective. Ms. Crilly recognises that trafficking comes down to economics and that it "makes financial sense". Conscious of the manner in which women are perceived by their traffickers, she describes the situation as the trafficker would:

> *If they [the pimps] can get the merchandise for nothing and make a profit, they will.*

In an interview, Sr. Onwunali revealed how drug traffickers are abandoning their engagement with the drugs world "to go into [human] trafficking", which is more profitable.[23] She describes how technological advancements have assisted in the fight against those transporting drugs, but how technology can never truly help in ascertaining the true circumstance of a person who is travelling. Technology cannot reveal whether the traveller is a victim of human trafficking. There is then an incentive to engage in lower risk activities that yield abundant reward.

So the very presence of prostitution, in a society that forbids it, is itself enough to attest to the relevance of a model that necessitates its association with human trafficking. There may be little point then in arguing that, in the face of even higher rewards and perhaps no additional risks, brothel operators would choose not to pursue the kind of behaviour they have already exhibited. When the lessons learned on a local scale are applied to the practice globally, the true extent of the problem begins to become apparent:

> *Some analysts believe that more money is made from trafficking women into prostitution than dealing in drugs, and the risk is*

lower. As a consequence, this is a boom area. Researchers make the point that drugs and guns are sold once, whereas women and girls can be repeatedly traded to clients.[24]

At the very least, there is ample reason to show why, on economics alone, one would reasonably support the case that the availability of prostitution in a society, legally or otherwise, is sufficient to conclude that "Prostitution ... contribute[s] to the phenomenon of trafficking in persons".[25]

---

1   George W. Bush Administration, 2003.
2   United States Department of State, 2005, p. 19.
3   Feingold, 2005, p. 28.
4   Vogel, 2011.
5   Collins and O'Shea, 2000, p. 5.
6   *Ibid.*, p. 4.
7   Ruhama, 2011, p. 4.
8   RTÉ Press Centre, 2012.
9   Davies, 2010.
10   *Criminal Law (Sexual Offences) Act, 1993.*
11   *Irish Examiner*, 2011.
12   Anti-Human Trafficking Unit, 2011, p. 29.
13   Kara, 2009, p. 40.
14   Organization for Security and Co-operation in Europe (OSCE), 2008, p.17.
15   International Labour Organization, 2005, p. 55.
16   United States Department of State, 2010, p. 7.
17   Kara, 2009, p. 22.
18   Escort Ireland, n.d.
19   Andrees, 2008, p. 30.
20   Jimmyjay, 2009.
21   silo, 2009.
22   Interview given August 2011.
23   Interview given September 2011.
24   Buckley, 2004, p. 31.
25   George W. Bush Administration, 2003.

CHAPTER 13
HUMAN TRAFFICKING IN IRELAND

Ireland's sex slaves "originate in Eastern Europe, Africa, including Nigeria, as well as South America and Asia". Those trafficked into conditions of forced labour "consist of men and women from Bangladesh, Pakistan, Egypt, and the Philippines, though there may also be some victims from South America, Eastern Europe, and other parts of Asia and Africa".[1]

In 2010, the Irish national police service, An Garda Síochána, investigated 69 cases of alleged human trafficking, involving 78 alleged victims. Sexual exploitation accounted for 72% of the victims, labour exploitation for just over 24% and the remainder alleged uncategorised exploitation.[2] Some 91% of the women brought into Ireland during this period had been trafficked for sexual exploitation,[3] while 27% of the trafficked were children.[4] An Garda Síochána reported that some victims had presented themselves to non-governmental organisations. Due to the cross-referral, some of those seen had presented themselves to both. However, the Anti-Human Trafficking Unit at the Department of Justice records that a total of 81 victims of trafficking presented themselves during 2010.[5] One must bear in mind that, as is the case with all figures relating to criminal activity, the figures never reveal the full extent of the crime. While the figure may not reveal the full extent of persons in Ireland under the control of traffickers, it does reveal the minimum threshold of the problem.

During the same period, Dublin-based charity Ruhama tended to 80 women who had been trafficked, as revealed in its annual report.[6] Women from Nigeria, Romania, Cameroon, Albania,

Moldova and Ghana accounted for 83% of the nationalities encountered.[7] Nigerian women account for 61% of the total.[8]

There were 40 arrests in 2010 in relation to trafficking in persons; 19 were made under the *Criminal Law (Human Trafficking) Act, 2008* and 21 under the *Child Trafficking and Pornography Act, 1998.*[9] The first convictions for offences of human trafficking also were secured during this time.[10]

Ms. Marion Walsh is Executive Director of Ireland's Anti-Human Trafficking Unit (AHTU) at the Department of Justice & Equality. An interview with Ms. Walsh provides preliminary figures for 2011, revealing that 57 victims were identified during the year; 44 of these were adults and 13 were children; 48 were female and nine were male; 38 had been trafficked for the purpose of sexual exploitation; 12 had been trafficked for labour exploitation and the remaining seven had been trafficked for combinations of the aforementioned.[11] When the final figures are released for 2011, more concrete analyses may be carried out. From the preliminary data available, Ms. Walsh noted that, when compared against the figures of the previous two years, there seems to be a trend showing a marked decline in the involvement of Africans as victims of human trafficking in Ireland. Conversely, the number of Eastern Europeans is rising steadily.

In 2011, the *Trafficking in Persons Report* description of trafficking in Ireland changed and a new term is now being used to describe human trafficking in Ireland. The description had remained pretty steady over preceding years with the removal and addition of the word 'transit' used to convey how people were being trafficked through Ireland, largely to the United Kingdom. In 2011, the report now declared Ireland:

> ... *a destination,* **source** *and transit country for women, men, and children subjected to sex trafficking and forced labor.*[12]

In an email to the author (August 2011), the U.S. Department of State attributed the recent change in Ireland's status to include the term "source" to the internal trafficking of Irish children for the purpose of prostitution. The *Trafficking in Persons Report* listed "Sligo, Kilkenny, Cork, and Dublin" as examples of where the exploitation occurs.[13] Bear in mind that the *Palermo Protocol* provides a separate definition for human trafficking where children are concerned. A person engaged in the "recruitment, transportation, transfer, harbouring or receipt of a child for the purpose of exploitation" is considered to have perpetrated an act of human trafficking.[14] Corroboration for the assertion that Irish children have been engaged in prostitution in Ireland is found in the annual report of Ireland's Anti-Human Trafficking Unit (AHTU). Its 2011 report reveals that, during the course of 2010, six Irish children were found to have been victims of human trafficking in Ireland.[15] All were trafficked for the purpose of sexual exploitation. Thus trafficking is a phenomenon that has not only affected Irish adults, as revealed earlier in this publication, but also Irish children.

Ireland is also a transit country for traffickers wishing to exploit the border with Northern Ireland to circumvent British immigration. The Ireland-Wales ferry service also features prominently as a point of entry.[16]

STORIES OF VICTIMS

The stories given by victims of trafficking in Ireland largely conform to what one would expect from accounts given elsewhere. An interview with Mary Crilly of Ireland's Sexual Violence Centre affirmed the relevance of debt as a significant means of control.[17] In effect, debt-bondage, a recognised method of slavery, is apparent amongst the victims of human trafficking in Ireland. Victims are kept in the dark with regard to the state of their account and doubtless it does not matter as it is merely a mechanism to exert control. According to Ms. Crilly, the enslaved "have no idea how much they owe or if they owe anything and that can go on for years". The debt can be further escalated by pimps by making claims upon the women that "now you have to pay for your food and your board". Other familiar methods of control are also evident, such as the seizure of travel documents. A woman, most victims usually are women, may see up to 12 men during the course of a single day. The account given by Ms. Crilly of the coercive forces is that they do not tend to be subtle, as might have been evidenced elsewhere. Instead the women are trapped in apartments and "they're watched 24 hours a day". The women also are moved from locality to locality to "meet the demand".

On the issue of prostitution, Ms. Crilly observes the manner in which the issue is framed. By focusing on the issue as prostitution rather than on the abuse that occurs within it, other considerations are drawn in. In effect, the sexual needs of the punter exceed all other considerations: "he needs it". The sexual needs of punters are given priority, with the implication that other concerns immediately become secondary at best. Thus a tolerance of prostitution emerges. Ironically, while society may be willing to tolerate punters availing of the services of prostitutes, she makes the point that it is the punters themselves who are unwilling to be associated with it. She notes too how tolerance does not extend to the sex workers themselves, wherever they may be. She is fully conscious of the implications for women who escape trafficking and the probability that they would be "demonised if they went back to their own village. They'd be ... seen as dirty ... not human anymore". Having endured so much, it is the raped woman who ends up ashamed. A two-fold process seems to be at play, in which the sexual needs of male punters are given priority while the women damaged by those needs are demonised and dismissed. In effect, in society "we're protecting the abusers all the time", she says.

Furthermore, Ms. Crilly sees no need to distinguish between the means by which the abuses came about. Many of the abuses perpetrated against victims of human trafficking are the same abuses perpetrated against prostitutes, yet Irish society distinguishes between them. Ms. Crilly does not entertain this distinction. Her focus is on the abuse, the consequences of which her organisation seeks to heal, rather on the means by which it was brought about. In drawing attention to how Irish society differentiates between certain abuses, she illuminates how a false distinction is being made when one scrutinises the situation from the perspective of the impact upon the victim. Exasperated, she poses the question:

> *How can a man in Ireland, knowing full well in his head, that this person is not 18, that this person has absolutely been trafficked and just do what he wants to do and throw the money there and walk away? .... and then rate her on the website [where she was advertised online]?*

She notes too that, while there are 1,000 women working in prostitution in Ireland today, few of them are Irish. Several sources claim, some citing Irish police sources, that as many as 90% of Ireland's prostitutes are not Irish.[18] The presence of non-nationals in circumstances of prostitution makes their engagement with that activity even more likely to be the result of human trafficking.

Considerable attention has been given to the issue of sexual exploitation of victims of trafficking in Ireland. Trafficking in Ireland, however, is not limited to only this form of abuse. Forced labour is also evident. The Migrant Rights Centre of Ireland (MRCI) reported the case of one foreign worker whose work permit was tied to his employer, as is the case with such permits in Ireland. Unscrupulous employers have an opportunity to manipulate the power they have over employees whose residency is dependent on their continued employment with their original employer. This form of exploitation is familiar to those acquainted with forced labour. In fact, changes have been made to these kinds of work permits in other countries, specifically to avoid these kinds of abuses. In Australia, a similar work permit system has attracted scrutiny for the same reasons. In the case detailed by the MRCI, the man was working as a chef in Dublin and he reported that, though he had been accustomed to work 70 hours per week, he was being paid only €250 per week, representing approximately only 40% of the minimum wage to which he was entitled.[19]

Another case reported by the MRCI was that of Nasir who worked as a qualified chef in Pakistan. An Irish customer at the restaurant where he worked commended Nasir on his cooking and offered him a job cooking in Ireland where he would be paid between €300 and €400 per week. Nasir accepted in the belief that a new life in Europe would be better than the one he was leaving behind. His new employer obtained the necessary work permit so Nasir could travel to Ireland and work there legally. On arrival in Ireland, he commenced work immediately. Nasir worked from 8:00am to 2:00am the following morning, seven days a week. He was given a one short break each day at 3:30pm. His duties were varied and included delivering the takeaway menus to housing estates, working as a chef, cleaning dishes, cleaning up after meals in the takeaway and delivering food to customers. His actual salary was at least €150 less than promised; he received €150 per week and his employer retained €100 of this as part of the cost of his work permit. It is estimated that deductions of €7,500 were made. Nassir's net €50 per week was a far cry from the promised €300 to €400 and the expectation that he would be treated fairly. Verbal abuse and threats of deportation were ever-present. Nasir's passport disappeared. Sometime later the restaurant business declined and Nasir left. His situation came to the attention of the local Gardaí following a minor accident and his stay in Ireland became tenuous as he possessed neither a passport nor a work or residence permit. The MRCI reported that it was attempting to help Nasir[20] and observed the presence of "abuse coupled with other subtle methods of coercion" in relation to this and other such cases.[21]

In 2008, An Garda Síochána established Operation Sibling as a joint initiative with the Romanian authorities to investigate allegations that Romanian nationals were being trafficked into Ireland for labour exploitation.[22] In late 2009, three men were convicted in Romania for their part in a crime syndicate that trafficked "28 people – including one child – into Co Wexford for labour exploitation".[23] Victims were regularly "threatened, beaten and sometimes held at gunpoint between 2006 and 2008".[24] The victims were employed in low paid jobs "and forced to repay debts of about €2,500 each".[25] One of the victims told the court that they "lived in constant fear".[26] Threats were made against them to the effect that the victim's "family and children would be killed".[27] The gang extorted most of the wages from the workers. The leader of the gang received seven years' imprisonment and his accomplices received five years each.[28]

The presence of forced labour has been observed amongst the house staff of diplomats residing in some countries. Diplomats may bring with them and their household a staff to manage their affairs. Domestic servants come to Ireland on working permits and may be subjected to the same abuses as other permitted workers. The *Trafficking in Persons Report 2011* notes in relation to Ireland that some forced labour "victims have been subjected to domestic servitude by foreign diplomats posted in Ireland".[29] In November 2010, Jamie Smyth of *The Irish Times* reported some "foreign diplomats in Ireland are taking unfair advantage of their domestic workers under the cloak of diplomatic immunity".[30] He detailed the case of Joan, who worked as a child-minder for a foreign diplomat and his family. Joan had worked for the diplomat's family in her native Africa prior to their move to Ireland. She recounted how everything changed very quickly after the diplomat's assignment to Ireland and their subsequent arrival; she was never let out of the home, was kept in a state of isolation and worked without pause. Despite being required to work seven days a week, she was never paid, except for one payment of €400 in 2008. The Gardaí acknowledged the difficulty associated with pursuing claims when the person against whom they are made is protected under the privilege of diplomatic immunity. The ICTU and MRCI have been lobbying government to implement safeguards specifically designed to prevent exactly this kind of abuse.[31]

One of the issues with which this publication is concerned is that of witchcraft. The case of Thomas Carroll was not the only such instance where an association with witchcraft is evident in the case of human trafficking. As mentioned earlier, Juju is being used in Ireland. The Anti-Human Trafficking Unit (AHTU) has reported that 13% of the human trafficking victims surveyed over a two-year period had been coerced by Juju. When this is adjusted to exclude non-Africans, the figure rises to 18%.[32] The AHTU's Executive Director Ms. Walsh appeals for sensitivity in relation to the issue and the importance of being aware of what it means to those who fall victim to its use:

> *When you understand that people subjected to this believe in it, it is useful to anybody dealing with potential victims to appreciate what this really means.*[33]

In July 2004, the decapitated body of Paiche Onyemaechi was pulled from the water near Brenar Bridge, Piltown, Co Kilkenny.[34] Early on, there were reports of an association with witchcraft.[35] Paiche had been missing for three weeks before the grim discovery of her fate was learned.[36] Certainly the press continues to maintain, at least until recently, that there was cause to believe there were links to witchcraft.[37] Her killers are believed to be Nigerian. Jim Cusack explains:

> *It is believed she was murdered and her head taken because she had either refused to return to work as a prostitute in a brothel, believed to have been in Kilkenny, or had not met debts to her traffickers. Her killers, believed to be Nigerians, have never been found, nor has the head.*[38]

One scandal concerns the number of children who go missing from State care.[39] For care professionals, the implications of a missing child go far beyond the image of the homeless runaway. In an interview, Ms. Mary Crilly said there is grave cause to be concerned about the plight of unaccompanied children who have entered Ireland only to disappear subsequently.[40] Some have been recovered, though most are still missing. Recent figures show that, between 2000 and 2010, some 512 children entered the country in this way and though some have been found, the number still missing is 440 children.[41] Considering what has been explored in relation to vulnerability, it is small wonder that Ms. Crilly believes "the worst has happened". Indeed the implication, she asserts, is that these children "have been trafficked or been killed". Information obtained from Wikileaks and subsequently reported in the press by journalists Tom Brady and Shane Phelan, supports that assessment:

> *According to the [Wikileaks] cable, Gardaí indicated trafficking gangs were increasingly targeting Ireland due to the ease with which children could escape from HSE facilities.*
>
> *Briefings received by the [U.S.] embassy between 2006 and 2008 indicated there was no evidence at the time to substantiate suspicions children were being trafficked into the sex trade in Ireland.*
>
> *However, for the past three years, the HSE has acknowledged in briefings with American officials that trafficking of minors into the sex trade is happening.[42]*

The following cases were recorded by the Children's Rights Alliance and properly belong here as they reflect the danger posed by traffickers to the welfare of children:

> *A 16-year-old Burundi girl came to the attention of Gardaí in Co. Louth after she was held captive in a house and abused. She had been taken from her home village in Africa at age 12 and inducted into sex slavery in different countries before being trafficked to Ireland.[43]*
>
> *A 16-year-old Romanian girl was trafficked to Ireland and controlled by a group of traffickers who locked her in a flat, together with other girls. She was forced to prostitute herself from 12pm to 4am. After the police raid, she was repatriated to Romania.[44]*

An underage female from Nigeria was found by Gardaí in a brothel in Kilkenny and was identified as a suspected victim of trafficking.[45]

A 17-year-old Sudanese girl was introduced to a Nigerian man by a family 'friend' who promised her an education in Europe. The man brought her to Dublin via Manchester and Belfast. While travelling, she was told to assume a Nigerian identity. She was given clothes and boots and a bag of condoms and was told to do anything that clients wanted. She was forced to have sex with a minimum of four men per night.[46]

There is then no reason to suppose that Ireland remains untouched by the issue of human trafficking. Many of the aspects encountered in Ireland reflect those found in other jurisdictions. Most abuse is accounted for by sexual exploitation and thereafter by forced labour. Women are the group predominantly exploited and thereafter children account for most of the remainder. In addition to being a destination for exploitation, Ireland is also a gateway for, and a source of, victims.

The multi-faceted nature of human trafficking in Ireland also is typical of that witnessed elsewhere. A thriving sex industry has created space for exploitative practices. Ireland has such an industry with 1,000 women working in prostitution daily. The presence of non-nationals in a nation's sex industry is more likely to exacerbate the problem, given the elevated vulnerability associated with migrant workers. Alarmingly, non-nationals play a significant role in Ireland's sex industry. Additional opportunities to exploit migrant workers have arisen in particular sectors and human trafficking has furnished workers to meet the demand. The creation of visas linking the holder's stay in the country to a specific employer has provided space for exploitation.

The primary realisation must be that human trafficking is today a problem in Ireland. The problem has already exhibited much of the fluidity demonstrated elsewhere, with its capacity to exploit different people for a variety of means. The secondary realisation is that the problem is an issue for communities. Victims are not confined to Ireland's largest cities. Instead traffickers will situate their victims wherever they can find a demand for them.

1   United States Department of State, 2011, p. 198.
2   Anti-Human Trafficking Unit, 2011, p. 8.
3   *Ibid.*, p. 9.
4   *Ibid.*, p. 10.
5   *Ibid. Note:* Of these 36 victims seen by charities and other NGOs, it is known that 28 have been referred to the Gardaí (hence they were included in the 78 victims total); information was unavailable on four; three had not been referred to the Gardaí; one was not contactable and there was no information on their whereabouts.
6   Ruhama, 2011, p. 10.
7   *Ibid.*, p. 10.
8   *Ibid.*, p. 10.
9   Anti-Human Trafficking Unit, 2011, p. 27.
10 *Ibid.*, p. 29.
11 Interview given February 2012.
12 United States Department of State, 2011, p. 198. Emphasis added.
13 *Ibid.*, p. 198.
14 United Nations Office on Drugs and Crime, 2004, p. 43.
15 Anti-Human Trafficking Unit, 2011, p. 37.
16 Children's Rights Alliance, 2010.
17 Interview given August 2011.
18 Baker, 2012; Cusack, 2010b.
19 Baker, 2010.
20 Migrant Rights Centre Ireland, 2006, pp. 23-24.
21 *Ibid.*, p. 26.
22 Department of Justice and Equality, 2011.
23 O'Brien, 2009.
24 *Ibid.*
25 *Ibid.*
26 *Ibid.*
27 *Ibid.*
28 Department of Justice and Equality, 2011.
29 United States Department of State, 2011, p. 198.
30 Smyth, 2010.

31   *Ibid.*
32   Anti-Human Trafficking Unit, 2011, p. 49.
33   Interview given February 2012.
34   Cusack, 2010a.
35   BBC News (UK), 2004.
36   RTÉ News (Ireland), 2004.
37   Cusack, 2010a.
38   *Ibid.*
39   Brady & Phelan, 2011.
40   Interview given August 2011.
41   Smyth, 2011.
42   Brady & Phelan, 2011.
43   Children's Rights Alliance, 2010.
44   *Ibid.*
45   *Ibid.*
46   *Ibid.*

CHAPTER 14
COUNTERMEASURES

Steps are being taken to address human trafficking in Ireland. In 2008, the Anti-Human Trafficking Unit (AHTU) was established in the Department of Justice, Equality & Law Reform.[1] The agency has several roles: "It has primary responsibility for co-ordinating policies and actions for government and non-governmental organisations".[2] Conscious of the importance of raising awareness on the issue, the AHTU researches and distributes information on human trafficking in Ireland.[3] Its Executive Director, Ms. Walsh, describes how central co-ordination is to the role of the AHTU.[4] It works with about 70 government NGOs and international organisations to deal with the issue of human trafficking on a variety of perspectives. She describes the approach as primarily consultative, one in which the AHTU drives Ireland's *National Action Plan*, which includes 144 actions. Every year, the AHTU engages in consultative processes to discuss the priority of actions listed in the plan. The role has evolved over time; the unit started out needing to create an environment where minimum standards had yet to be attained in areas such as accommodation, legal aid and healthcare.

LEGISLATION AND INTERNATIONAL SUPPORT

Specific legislation was introduced to address human trafficking in Ireland. The *Criminal Law (Human Trafficking) Act, 2008* complements existing legislation and "provides for offences of trafficking in adults and children".[5] The manner in which the act of trafficking is defined in the legislation is consistent with the definition laid out in the *Palermo Protocol*.[6] The legislation introduced the possibility of life imprisonment for trafficking-related offenses. Five years' imprisonment and/or an unlimited fine may be imposed on a punter who knowingly avails of the services of a trafficked person.[7]

Pre-existing legislation also forms part of the framework applied to tackling trafficking. Legislation such as the *Child Trafficking and Pornography Act, 1998* and *the Sexual Offences (Jurisdiction) Act, 1996* may be applied to cases of sexual exploitation. Abuses inflicted through trafficking for the purpose of labour exploitation may be addressed through the *Organisation and Working Time Act, 1997* and the *National Minimum Wage Act, 2000*.[8]

Of course, trafficking is not all about the offence. The victim is the most important element of the practice. This is reflected in Ireland's forthcoming *Immigration, Residence and Protection Bill*, which is currently working its way through the legislative process. When it is implemented, the legislation will allow victims of trafficking a *recovery and reflection* period of 60 days.[9] The intention is to allow victims to reside in Ireland for some time after their victimisation so that the process of recovery can begin. Additionally, the measure is intended to facilitate the investigation of the crimes perpetrated against the victim. One of the difficulties encountered by police authorities in investigating crimes against illegal migrants is that the exposure of the crime also exposes their illegal status. Situations occur where victims of trafficking are summarily deported. Aside from the implications for the victim, investigating the crime becomes futile in the absence of the complainant and the testimony they might provide. The new legislation will permit the Minister for Justice to grant a temporary residence permit where:

> ... *the permission is necessary for the purposes of allowing the foreign national to continue to assist An Garda Síochána or other relevant authorities in relation to any investigation or prosecution arising in relation to the trafficking.*[10]

Changes have been implemented within the organisation of An Garda Síochána itself. The Garda National Immigration Bureau (GNIB) now has a specialist unit section dedicated to investigating cases of human trafficking.[11]

Ireland ratified the *UN Convention against Transnational Organised Crime* and the *Protocol to Prevent, Suppress, and Punish Trafficking in Persons, especially Women and Children* in June 2010.[12] Ireland also has implemented the measures required under the *European Union Council Framework Decision 2002/629/JHA on Combating Trafficking in Human Beings (2002)* and has signed the *Council of Europe Convention on Action against Trafficking in Human Beings (2005)*.[13]

Measures to counter human trafficking are sometimes referred to as the '3Ps': Prevention, Protection and Prosecution.[14] The creation of the AHTU, the drafting of Ireland's *National Action Plan* and the introduction of legislation should be viewed as deliberate measures taken by the Irish State to implement a 3Ps response. Indeed the *National Action Plan to Prevent and Combat Trafficking of Human Beings in Ireland 2009-2012*, another key measure in Ireland's efforts to combat trafficking, acknowledges the inspiration it draws from the 3Ps.[15] The items detailed here are but some of the measures undertaken as part of the plan.

These measures become more than mere bureaucracy. Journalist Stephen Rogers reported on some of the actions taken by Irish authorities in recent times. He notes:

> More than 400 operational gardaí have received detailed training to enable them identify and refer victims of human trafficking for support and deal with prosecutions, if appropriate.
>
> A further 2,674 personnel have received awareness raising training as part of the final phase of their training. That training is now part of the final phase of training for all Garda recruits.
>
> Senior Garda personnel have been trained in techniques specific to the investigation of human trafficking related crimes.[16]

Just as Ireland's approach links with a broader international philosophy on how the problem ought to be tackled, it also is encouraged by international actors. The U. S. Department of State, in particular its Office to Monitor and Combat Trafficking in Persons, actively scrutinises, comments and coerces, if necessary, countries to act on this international philosophy. The product of this work is embodied in the annual *Trafficking in Persons Report*. Thus momentum is attained and maintained. Countries are rated on their efforts and those failing to meet the requirements set forth face the possibility of international sanction by the United States government. Furthermore, the United States cautions that it may oppose assistance by the World Bank and the International Monetary Fund to those same nations.[17]

Awareness is not only important for authorities, it is important that the public also are aware of human trafficking. To this end, the Blue Blindfold campaign is being promoted by authorities in the United Kingdom and Ireland as part of their efforts to combat trafficking in persons. The campaign's main UK website is available at **http://www.blueblindfold.co.uk**, while the Irish equivalent is available at **http://www.blueblindfold.gov.ie/**. The message of the campaign is one of awareness that the issue of human trafficking is not a far-off phenomenon and that communities need to be aware of its likely presence in their areas. The websites provide details of indicators of victimhood. There has been criticism that the campaign has not had a higher profile, given its supposed role in raising awareness of the issue as part of Ireland's national plan.[18]

THE DIGNITY PROJECT

Trafficking occurs internally to the borders of a State and sometimes across those borders. Cooperation with authorities and organisations in other jurisdictions in such cases is important. One such initiative was undertaken by Dublin Employment Pact (DEP). In 2008, DEP successfully applied for EU Daphne funding. This EU fund is specifically targeted at countering violence against women. The Dignity Project, a partnership of state bodies and NGOs, resulted. In an interview, Philip O'Connor, Director of the DEP, recalls how success in obtaining EU funding was accompanied by success in securing national sources of funding.[19] Additional monies were obtained from State authorities, including the Department of Justice, the Garda National Immigration Bureau (GNIB) and the Health Services Executive (HSE). A consortium of State bodies and NGOs thus was established. Partners included the Anti-Human Trafficking Unit (AHTU) of the Department of Justice, the HSE, FÁS, the Irish Legal Aid Board, the Immigrant Council of Ireland, Ruhama, Sonas Housing and others.

The primary aim was the establishment of an interagency framework to help victims who had been trafficked for the purpose of sexual exploitation. The project goal was achieved through the establishment of a memorandum of understanding between the NGOs and State agencies participating in the consortium. The memorandum permitted these agencies to coordinate their activities, increasing the efficiency and quality with which services were delivered, so as to enhance the overall level of service available to the victims of sex trafficking. Core services include the provision of secure accommodation, an absolute necessity for those seeking to escape the clutches of traffickers and vital access to health and legal services. With the support of FÁS, Ruhama operated training workshops. Thirty women undertook the workshops, with 28 completing them; 90% were African victims of trafficking, all of them were trafficked into Ireland for the purpose of sexual exploitation.

While the main body of work was conducted in Ireland, there were three international partners with whom the Dignity Project engaged. Mr. O'Connor recalls that it was the partnership with the city of Madrid that provided the inspiration for the creation of "pathways out of prostitution". The result was the creation of training workshops that played an important role in preparing former prostitutes for new careers. The partnership with Glasgow

Community & Safety Services brought with it the opportunity to strengthen the relationship between Glasgow's Strathclyde Police and An Garda Síochána. The final partnership was that with Klaipèda Social Psychological Service Centre in Lithuania. This too brought a relationship with NGOs and the local police. As a major port, the city of Klaipèda has ample experience in dealing with the issue of human trafficking.

Aside from the reactionary aspect associated with looking after the needs of victims, the Dignity Project also looked at more proactive measures. It was the exploration of arrangements in Sweden that proved most fruitful in this regard. The Swedish government provided the project with an English translation of a document detailing its approach (available from the Dignity Project website at **http://www.dublinpact.ie/dignity/**), which had been so effective in reducing the numbers working as prostitutes. According to Mr. O'Connor, there are 15,000 prostitutes in Barcelona and only 200 in Stockholm, a city of comparable size. Legislation is effective because changes introduced in 1999 now criminalise the client and not the sex worker.

Through the efforts of the Dignity Project, protocols were established for identifying and dealing with likely victims as well as affording them opportunities to escape their traffickers. The close relationship with the Swedish Government yielded a new focus, one emphasising the need to prosecute the client rather than the sex worker. The results of the work were passed on to the then Minister for consideration. The present Minister, Mr. Alan Shatter TD, has responded to parliamentary questions on the approach of prosecuting the buyer of sex. This is an approach better known as the Swedish Model. Minister Shatter outlined the situation thus:

In 2010, the Swedish Government completed an evaluation of its 1999 legislation criminalising the purchase of sex. The Dignity Project arranged a visit to Sweden ... My Department's Anti-Human Trafficking Unit and the Garda National Immigration Bureau were partners with observer status.

I will be examining a report prepared by my Department following the visit to Stockholm and which was submitted to the Attorney General's Office. I will also be examining the Attorney's recent advices concerning the legal and constitutional implications of introducing a ban on the purchase of sex.[20]

The role of demand and the fact that this demand is capable of sustaining the activities of an estimated 1,000 prostitutes in Ireland today was explored earlier. There is increasingly an appreciation of the significance of this point and, given this understanding, it can hardly be surprising that in time the focus would fall not upon the sex worker but on the consumer. One Irish campaign, entitled *Turn Off the Red Light*, is focusing entirely on the issue of demand. The campaign should not be confused with a counter-campaign entitled *Turn Off the Blue Light*, which purports to be an alliance of sex workers. The former campaign, *Turn Off the Red Light*, has a stated objective of ending "prostitution and sex trafficking in Ireland."[21] The campaign is a collaboration of a significant number of organisations, including the Dublin Rape Crisis Centre, Rape Crisis Network Ireland, Barnardo's, the Migrant Rights Centre Ireland, the Immigrant Council of Ireland, the National Women's Council of Ireland, Ruhama and Stop Sex Trafficking to name but a few. The campaign's website is **http://www.turnofftheredlight.ie**.

---

[1]   Kelleher *et al.*, 2009, p. 124.

[2]   Department of Justice, Equality & Law Reform, n.d., p. 50.

[3]   *Ibid.*, p. 50.

[4]   Interview given February 2012.

[5]   Walsh, n.d., p. 3.

[6]   *Criminal Law (Human Trafficking) Act, 2008*, p. 7; United Nations Office on Drugs and Crime, 2000, p. 42.

[7]   Walsh, n.d., p. 3.

[8]   Department of Justice, Equality & Law Reform, n.d., p. 9.

[9]   *Immigration, Residence & Protection Bill, 2010*, p. 171.

[10]   *Ibid.*, p. 170.

[11]   *Irish Examiner*, 2011.

[12] Department of Justice & Equality, 2010.

[13] Department of Justice, Equality & Law Reform, n.d., p. 36-37.

[14] United Nations Office on Drugs and Crime, n.d.

[15] Department of Justice, Equality & Law Reform, n.d., p. 6.

[16] Rogers, 2011b.

[17] United States Department of State, 2011, p. 14.

[18] Department of Justice, Equality & Law Reform, n.d., p. 63.

[19] Interview given June 2011.

[20] Shatter, 2011.

[21] Turn Off The Red Light, n.d.

CHAPTER 15
UNDOING AND RE-DOING THE SELF

The victimhood of sex slaves can end in many ways. For some, the pain may become too much and the end comes in the form of suicide.[1] For others, the violence ends in a final violent act of murder.[2] Others escape through the help of a sympathetic punter, or *via* a fleeting moment of self-reliance on the part of the victim at an opportune time, or through the intervention of the authorities in the form of police raids. In a final act of contempt, it has been known for traffickers to throw their victims out onto the street when they have outlasted their usefulness and become a burden upon their exploiter. This usually occurs when "more attractive (usually meaning younger) victims" have been acquired to take their place.[3]

Victims who emerge from trafficking face an assortment of worldly challenges such as physical security from the trafficker, accommodation, financial needs, health issues including the risk of STDs, issues of psychological and spiritual health, legal issues around residency and those legal issues concerning testimony. Some of the symptoms and risks victims may encounter are anger and rage, sense of loss of control, hypervigilance, sleep disorders, shame, depression, lack of interest, terror, post traumatic stress disorder (PTSD) and suicide.[4] All of these matters are important considerations in providing care for victims of human trafficking but the list is deficient in one very important regard. It tells us little about the inner world, the psychology and spiritual mindset of the victim. Finding a voice to give expression to the real effects of abuse might reasonably be considered a formidable challenge. Yet it is not a futile exercise. There are voices wishing to be heard and one of these is the voice of Susan Brison. The context of her tale is different but the implications are the same.

On a beautiful summer's day in 1990 in the south of France, Susan Brison decided to take a walk. On the day on which Americans celebrate their independence, 4 July, she was to lose hers. On a lonely road, she was attacked, beaten and raped. After her attacker was done, he tried, repeatedly, to murder her. Eventually, he left her for dead. Amidst the chaos of the events of the days and months that followed, the inner turmoil that she was experiencing was not at all evident. Long after the demands of the world, her medical care and the police investigation had been placated, her inner world was still one filled with pain.

Today Susan Brison is an Associate Professor at Dartmouth College in New Hampshire. In her book, *Aftermath: Violence and the Remaking of a Self*, Brison gives an extraordinarily frank account of the attack and the "unimaginably painful aftermath of violence".[5] She develops a "view of the self", one that is "capable of being undone by violence" and finds meaning in the words of French writer Charlotte Delbo: "I died in Auschwitz, but no one seems to know it".[6]

Brison outlines the implications of violence for the person upon whom it is perpetrated, the possibility that a person, in effect can be undone, a process she describes as an "undoing of the self".[7] The undoing of the self is so profound that one now has "a different relationship" with one's own body. The body becomes "a site of increased vulnerability".[8] As the body becomes this font of pain, victims find "ways of disassociating themselves from their bodies".[9] In so doing, the victim not only alienates themselves from their self, but also severs "the sustaining connection between the self and the rest of humanity".[10] The trauma that so prevailed in its conquest of the body consequentially prevailed in its dominance of the mind, making the distinction between body and mind become negligible. Escape from the body to the mind, for Brison, thus was denied. In her own words, "I was no longer the same person I had been before the assault".[11]

In very similar words, Mary Crilly of Ireland's Sexual Violence Centre says, "I think it destroys … [the victims] … I think it destroys their soul".[12] She talks of people who are trafficked into Ireland only to be raped several times a day and, in her expert opinion, the victims, usually women, are "destroyed from the inside out". In words very similar to those used by Brison, she describes how under these circumstances, everything is taken from the person, even "her being has been taken".

Dr. Brison's and Ms. Crilly's words may give greater meaning to those uttered by victims of violence in general but also to victims of trafficking where violence plays such a central role. Against the backdrop of this understanding, the words of one 15 year-old Chinese girl, rescued from her traffickers in England, attain deeper meaning:

> It's always going to be there, part of me. In the beginning you feel like you had [to] fight but after, you just switch off. I know it sounds crazy but you just switch off. You're like a robot.[13]

The description given by this girl of her experience, in which she likens herself to a robot, can be reconciled with descriptions of Sr. Onwunali's work in Italy.[14] Sr. Onwunali describes how many of the victims she has encountered "don't have human feelings". Life has been emptied and "they don't value things because of the trauma". She asks whether it could be otherwise: "what do you think they are going to be [like]" having worked in prostitution?

Several consequences flow from an appreciation of the fact that a person indeed can be undone. The first of these relates to the care of victims. While the victim may have been freed of the environment in which violence had been perpetrated against them, this is not to say that they are freed of the effects of violence. Their inner life may continue to be one filled with pain and turmoil long after they have been physically freed from their captors. In Brison's case, all the outwardly measures were attended to but perhaps the most important consideration, that of her inner world, was neglected.

Another consequence of the undoing of the self is the validation it provides to the view that human traffickers employ violence to gain full control over their victims. Violence is at the heart of human trafficking, regardless of whether the intended purpose is forced labour, sexual exploitation or some other end. Exploiters have learned, whether through instinct, experience or both, how violence may be used to fashion compliant human beings. Earlier in this book, the reader was advised to observe not only *what is done*, but also *why it is done* in relation to the use of violence. The purpose was to illustrate how violence is used to serve some purpose other than an expression of mere contempt. When the issue of violence is addressed again, this time from the point of view of the impact violence has on its victim, it becomes appreciable just how effective those tactics can be. The rape and near-murder of Susan Brison meant that she was undone as a person, made powerless and felt isolated from the rest of humanity. This is exactly the effect that the trafficker seeks in employing violence and we have seen from two perspectives, the act and the impact, how this is so.

Counsellors providing care to the victims of human trafficking appreciate that, while a victim has been freed from the clutches of the trafficker, they may not yet be free of the trafficker's influence. One of the factors visited in the course of this work was the use of witchcraft and the manner in which it may be employed to control persons. During the course of her work in Italy, Sr. Onwunali has sometimes observed how, even in the first week of escape, the girls often cannot sleep due to the sense of impending doom associated with breaking their oath. Even the very opening of a door can be enough to provoke a startled response. Control can transcend physical proximity. The trafficker need not be near at hand to make his presence felt. A combination of fear and powerlessness may compel the victim to feel that they have no more autonomy after their release than they had before it. The psychological restraints remain intact. The psychological impact can be profound on those who violate their oaths and this likely produces the mental instability that some violators suffer. The consequence is that this only serves to perpetuate the potency of Juju.

All of these factors attest to the potency of violence as a tactic. Not only are victims controlled through violence but paradoxically, even if they manage to escape, the violence, far from being a deterrent to return, actually can bind the victim to their exploiter. One consequence is the very real risk of the victim returning to their trafficker. Another risk is that the victim seeks to escape their misery through suicide.

One vital question to consider at this point is whether the mental imagery conveyed by the very term human trafficking adequately reflects reality? Having explored the issue and having gained insight into the motives and tactics of traffickers, how does one imagine the appearance of a victim? Do acts of kidnapping adequately account for most of what occurs in human trafficking? Is it necessary to find the victim shackled to a bed in a locked room to categorise them as genuine victims? It is only through an understanding of the methods, motives and impact of human trafficking that one can appreciate it for what is. The image of the victim of human trafficking bound by physical restraints becomes less important. Only those who are in possession of their self, their own will, need to be physically restrained. In one Australian case, the judge, Justice McInerney, was able to grasp the truth of the situation before him and, in making his judgement, he found:

> ... that due to a combination of circumstances, each alleged victim, while not locked in the premises, was "effectively restrained by the insidious nature of their contract".[15]

Victims are not always hidden away from view in darkened rooms. Holland, where prostitution was legalised, provides one of the best examples of this. A case described earlier in this publication, in which at least one Irish national was trafficked for the purpose of sexual exploitation, was known as the Sneep case. A Turkish gang ran a human trafficking operation involving over 120 women from

Eastern Europe and the Netherlands.[16] The case was considered remarkable, given that it was a large-scale human trafficking operation in such a high-visibility environment; the women were prostituted *via* "licensed window prostitution".[17] The victims were put on public display and the more public they were, the less anyone thought to consider the possibility they had been trafficked. Things are not always what they seem. Apparently consensual arrangements may not be consensual at all. This demonstrates how the tactics employed by traffickers are far more advanced than the social narrative used to describe their methods. To speak of the worst abuses of human trafficking as being "underground" could be construed to have missed the point. The worst abuses can be readily perpetrated in plain sight if one understands the essence of human trafficking and the centrality of violence to its methods. It is for reasons such as these that the U.S. Department of State has called for a more "sophisticated understanding of the realities on the ground ... to ensure that ... trafficking victims are not wrongly discounted as consenting adults".[18]

In concluding, it is important to acknowledge that, even in the darkness of despair, there is still room for hope. The self can be remade and Brison points to the dependence of trauma survivors "on empathic others who are willing to listen to their narratives".[19] Ms. Crilly echoes the sentiment in stating that the rebuilding of the person is achieved not primarily through the intervention of external actors but through the efforts of the victim themselves. People "know what they want and what they don't want", she says and this is an important consideration in realising that the direction of care can come from the person themselves rather than being something imposed. In this way, Ms. Crilly emphasises the importance of "listening and really listening", especially that given during their time as victims of violence they are not accustomed to being listened to.[20]

There are many perspectives one can take in an examination of human trafficking. Many have been explored here to help the reader gain a deeper appreciation of the phenomenon. Effort has been made to illuminate the true essence of human trafficking even unto capturing its very spirit. In parting, the words of Susan Brison are offered in relation to her own ordeal as they seem to convey the spirit of human trafficking best:

> *It is as if the tormentor says with his blows, "You are nothing but a body, a mere object for my will".*[21]

[1]   Olaniyi, 2003, p. 50.

[2]   *Ibid.*, p. 50.

[3]   Lee, 2007, p. 102.

[4]   Brison, 2002, pp. 40-90.

[5]   *Ibid.*, p. x.

[6]   Quoted in *ibid.*, p. xi.

[7]   *Ibid.*, p. 39.

[8]   *Ibid.*, p. 44.

[9]   *Ibid.*, p. 47.

[10]   *Ibid.*, p. 44.

[11]   *Ibid.*, p. 44.

[12]   Interview given August 2011.

[13]   Channel 4, 2010a.

[14]   Interview given September 2011.

[15]   David, 2008, p. 54.

[16]   United States Department of State, 2011, p. 273; Siegel, 2009, p. 9.

[17]   Siegel, 2009, p. 9.

[18]   United States Department of State, 2011, p. 24.

[19]   Brison, 2002, p. 62.

[20]   Interview given August 2011.

[21]   Brison, 2002, p. 47.

CONCLUSION

The Church has always had the duty of scrutinizing the signs of the times and of interpreting them in the light of the Gospel.[1]

Human trafficking and the enslaving influence of witchcraft that sometimes goes with it are among the most negative of these signs. Previous chapters have attempted to interpret them, here we point towards needed responses to the enslavement they bring.

This book shows how today, just like in 1631 when Murat Reis sold the people of Baltimore into the slave markets of Algiers, the process is fuelled by the greed of the trafficker and the demand of those who would use, abuse and exploit their fellow human beings for economic benefit or their own gratification. However, victims are not only people carried off to far-away lands, they also live here among us. Slavery exists in Ireland today. Many are immigrants who were brought here but, as these chapters have shown, Irish men, women and children in recent times also have been victims of human trafficking. Ireland is a source country that supplies victims of trafficking, a destination country that receives them and also a gateway through which trafficked persons pass from one country to another. Equally shocking is the reality that we, Irish people, are fuelling the demand that enslaves.

As a Catholic Church-based organisation, Cois Tine looks to the principles of Catholic Social Teaching for guidance. A primary principle of this teaching is belief in the fundamental dignity of every human person. Human trafficking and control through witchcraft deny and seek to destroy this dignity. Implicit in the fundamental dignity of every human person is the requirement that, on the level of society, every law, policy, programme and priority be measured and evaluated by whether it enhances or diminishes human life and dignity. In responding to human trafficking and witchcraft, our procedures, actions and methods must measure up to this standard.

Other guiding principles of Catholic Social Teaching are the *common good* and *solidarity*. The common good is "the sum total of social conditions which allow people, either as groups or as individuals, to reach their fulfilment more fully and more easily".[2] The principle of solidarity highlights the equality of all in dignity and rights and also interdependence between individuals and peoples.[3] The enslavement that is inherent to human trafficking and the controlling use of witchcraft is contrary to these principles. Therefore programmes to educate, prevent, raise awareness, as well as interventions that care for and protect those who have been trafficked, are appropriate responses. These respect human dignity, show solidarity and promote the common good. Such responses can, and should, involve individuals, society, faith-based organisations and the State. In essence, such responses seek to re-empower victims and also to address the root causes and consequences of their enslavement by trafficking and witchcraft.

The State has a particular role in addressing the issue of human trafficking and also in preparing its agents to encounter the witchcraft that may accompany it. "The responsibility for attaining the common good, besides falling to individual persons, belongs also to the State, since the common good is the reason that the political authority exists."[4] Laws, policies and procedures, along with the expertise, training and the resources to implement them, are the responsibility of the State. Further, the institutions of the State are best placed to facilitate and promote means and procedures to identify and report incidents of trafficking as well as campaigns and education to raise awareness of its causes and effects.

The apprehension and appropriate punishment of traffickers are also essential parts of the State's role, as are the provision of support and the rehabilitation of victims. While the Irish State has made great progress over the past decade in respect of legislation and policing, there is still need for a more victim-centred approach. The need to prosecute the trafficker and to support and rehabilitate its victims must be kept in balance. The State too has the power to enact practical measures that will prevent the exploitation and abuse of those trafficked for prostitution. Two such measures highlighted in this book should be given further consideration: the criminalisation of the purchase of sex and the shutting down of advertised mobile phone numbers that are being used to facilitate the sex trade. As human trafficking is fuelled by greed and demand, practical measures that will reduce profitability for traffickers and make legal penalties more likely for punters (those who use prostitutes) will help reduce the demand for trafficked persons.

Church and faith groups also have a role in combating trafficking that is totally consistent with "the Church's mission for the redemption of the human race and its liberation from every oppressive situation".[5] Faith groups, through their structures, are ideally placed to play a major role in raising awareness of trafficking and of the means to combat and report it. Church groups and organisations also can provide practical pastoral support and care for both victims of trafficking and witchcraft that assists in their rehabilitation.

For pastoral workers in Ireland, the encounter of witchcraft or magic is a new and perplexing phenomenon. Guidance from Africans perhaps can help in pointing to a response to the person who comes seeking spiritual support. Fr. Clement Majawa, a Malawian academic, says: "Since Christ in the Gospels encountered the Devil, it is proper for Christians to accept the reality of witchcraft".[6] Pastoral workers need to come to terms with the African worldview, which accepts the existence of evil powers. The views of the Kenyan theologian Fr. Michael Katola bring us a step further when he says, "It is important for the Church to understand the fears of the people and not to attribute them to superstition".[7] He goes on to say that, "Many of our Christians seek deliverance, healing and exorcism from other denominations because priests do not realise they have redemptive powers".[8] In African communities, the traditional healer had a valued role. Greater use of the healing ministry of the Church can be made in responding to victims of witchcraft. In order to support and facilitate a caring and spiritual response, work needs to be done in Ireland to develop guidelines and resources for pastoral workers to consult and use.

In addition to spiritual support, appropriate social and psychological care for victims is paramount. Following sex trafficking experiences, women and girls who have already suffered abuse and disempowerment must then deal with police, immigration authorities, the stigma of sex work, cooperating with an investigation and the possibility of putting themselves or their families in danger by doing so. This may be made even more stressful if there are fears associated with the breaking of witchcraft oaths and the supernatural retribution they believe this will call down. Victims also may have concerns about returning to their families, who may be unaware of their experiences or who may be aware and consequently be unwelcoming. In addition and not least, they also will have to face the same concerns that caused them to leave home in the first place.

The ability to form a trusting relationship with the trafficked person that reduces shame and fear of judgement is essential. Maintaining confidentiality will be very important in building this trust. The need for confidentiality in dealing with those who fall victim to witchcraft has already been made very clear elsewhere in this book (see **Part One**, *Witchcraft and Modernity in Africa*, and also *African Witchcraft in the Irish Context*). For those working with individuals who have suffered from trafficking or witchcraft, a good rule of thumb to adopt would be: *It is not for me to pass judgement but to seek to understand, learn from and respect the beliefs and dignity of the person before me so that they can again see this dignity in themselves.* The experience of witchcraft is, for those who are victimised, a very real one that a pastoral worker or service provider has no right to deny, judge or disregard.

Many Westerners, theologians, psychologists, etc. do deny the existence of witchcraft. But for many Africans, it is something that permeates every aspect of their lives. Denying or laughing at such beliefs will not help the victim. However, it will stop people talking about their experience. Perhaps the most constructive approach, reported earlier in this book, is that adopted by German police where "the first step in contact with women who have been exposed to controlling Voodoo rituals is to show acceptance, thus it is only when confidence has been built up that women talk about what they have gone through".[9] This book highlights the relationship between witchcraft and trafficking. Through this relationship, an invisible chain of self-imposed compliance, that ties the victim to the trafficker, is forged. The reader, however, should try to appreciate that witchcraft also has a wider impact that affects the lives of many Africans in ways not associated with trafficking. These, as Dr. DeWan has pointed out, can be both good and bad. Sorcery and magic are used also to cure, to counter evil and to put wrongs to right as well as to inflict evil and suffering.

It is hard to prescribe a general response, as each case is unique and requires careful, individual assessment. Indeed the tailoring of such an individual response may well be key to the recovery of each victim. However, as stated above, with every individual, it is essential to listen in a non-judgemental way. This is the first step in enabling a caring response to the very real cultural, psychological and spiritual impacts experienced by the victim.

The prophet Ezekiel (11.19) foretold that time when the heart of stone would be transformed, replaced with a heart of flesh and a new spirit. Upholding the principles of human dignity, solidarity and the common good are a means of bringing this transformation about in ourselves. They call us beyond the geographic boundaries of our island and beyond the barriers of race, ethnicity, gender, economic status and nationality, inviting us to see ourselves as members of one global family – brothers and sisters whose fate and well-being are tied together. They call us to an awareness of our own values and prejudices and of how these inform the way we interact with people whose experience of life is so different that we find them difficult to relate to. They also challenge us to respect difference and to attempt actively to understand the diverse cultural backgrounds of people we encounter. Through the guidance of these principles, we can undergo a self-transformation that will establish, in us, that heart of flesh which will provide the foundation for effectively identifying and responding both to human trafficking and the witchcraft that sometimes accompanies it.

As individuals, groups, Church and State, we all have a role in transforming or 're-doing the self' of those enslaved by witchcraft and trafficking. We hope that this book will help readers to understand the causes and effects of human trafficking and witchcraft and also encourage discussion and further research. Ultimately, we hope it will help to bring about a caring response that will restore dignity and undermine the violent and unjust enslavement that diminishes our human family.

Angelo Lafferty SMA and Gerard Forde

---

[1]   Pope Paul VI, 1965.
[2]   Pontifical Council for Justice and Peace, 2004, para. 164.
[3]   *Ibid.*, para. 193.
[4]   *Ibid.*, para. 168.
[5]   World Synod of Catholic Bishops, 1971.
[6]   Catholic Information Service for Africa (CISA), 2007.
[7]   *Ibid.*
[8]   *Ibid.*
[9]   Polisen, 2010, p. 12.

BIBLIOGRAPHY

AFP (2005). 'Six arrested over grisly ritual killings in Indonesia', available: http://www.smh.com.au/news/world/six-arrested-over-grisly-ritual-killings-in-indonesia/2005/08/07/1123353204100.html [Accessed 24 August 2011].

African Women's Development Fund (2011). '"The Witches of Gambaga': A documentary by Yaba Badoe', African Women's Development Fund Blog, 20 January [Accessed 16 February 2012].

Al Jazeera (2011). 'People and power: The Nigerian connection', available: http://english.aljazeera.net/programmes/peopleandpower/2011/08/2011 89141348631784.html [Accessed 22 August 2011].

Allen, C. (2009b). 'White witch: Helen Barrett', *Cork Independent*, 29 October, available: http://www.corkindependent.com/profiles/profiles/white-witch:-helen-barrett [Accessed 22 February 2011].

Allen, J. Jr. (2009a). 'Condemned by Pope, witchcraft a reality in Africa', *National Catholic Reporter*, 21 March, available: http://ncronline.org/print/12657 [Accessed 8 March 2012].

Amnesty International (2005). 'Dirty, degrading and dangerous', available: http://www.amnesty.org/en/library/asset/ACT30/027/2005/en/ca1dd0b3-d470-11dd-8743-d305bea2b2c7/act300272005en.pdf [Accessed 22 August 2011].

Andrees, B. & Belser, P. (2009). *Forced Labor: Coercion and Exploitation in the Private Economy,* Boulder, CO: Lynne Rienner Publishers.

Andrees, B. (2008). 'Forced labour and trafficking in Europe: How people are trapped in, live through and come out', *InFocus Programme on Promoting the Declaration*, No. 57.

Anti-Human Trafficking Unit (2011). *Annual Report of Trafficking in Human Beings in Ireland for 2010*, Dublin: Department of Justice & Equality.

Ariadne, R. (2007). 'African witchcraft – The history, the practices, and the controversies', *Articlebase.com*, available: http://www.articlesbase.com/

religion-articles/african-witchcraft-the-history-the-practices-and-the-controversies-269927.html [Accessed 6 August 2011].

Ariyo, D. (2005). 'We must change 'witch' practices'', BBC News, 4 June, available: http://news.bbc.co.uk/2/hi/uk_news/england/london/4609355.stm [Accessed 21 February 2011].

Aronowitz, A., Theuemann, G. & Tyurkanova, E. (2010). 'Analysing the business model of trafficking in human beings to better prevent the crime', OSCE Office of the Special Representative and Co-ordinator for Combating Trafficking in Human Beings, available: http://www.osce.org/cthb/69028 [Accessed 29 July 2011].

Aronowitz, A.A. (2001). 'Smuggling and trafficking in human beings: The phenomenon, the markets that drive it and the organisations that promote it', *European Journal on Criminal Policy and Research*, Vol. 9, No. 2, pp. 163-195.

Aronowitz, A.A. (2009). *Human Trafficking, Human Misery: The Global Trade in Human Beings*, Westport, CT: Praeger.

Ashforth, A. (2001). 'AIDS, witchcraft, and the problem of power in post-apartheid South Africa', in *Occasional Papers 10: Thursday Seminar*, Princeton, NJ: School of Social Science, Institute for Advanced Study.

Associated Press (2008). 'Indonesia executes man convicted of killing 42 people in ritual slayings', 11 July, available: http://www.foxnews.com/story/0,2933,380421,00.html [Accessed 24 August 2011].

Austen, R. (1993). 'Moral economy of witchcraft: An essay in comparative history', in: Comaroff, J.C.A.J. (ed.), *Modernity and Its Malcontents*, Chicago: University of Chicago Press, pp. 89-110.

Bahman, Z. (2010). 'I put a spell on you', *New Internationalist*, Issue 436 (October), available: http://www.newint.org/features/2010/10/01/afghanistan-sorcery-women/ [Accessed 20 October 2010].

Baker, N. (2010). 'Poll supports changes to work permit system', *Irish Examiner*, 29 September 2010.

Baker, N. (2012). 'Calls to make buying sex a criminal offence', *Irish Examiner*, 3 February, available: http://www.irishexaminer.com/ireland/calls-to-make-buying-sex-a-criminal-offence-144048.html [Accessed 18 February 2012].

Baltimore Heritage Limited (n.d.). 'The sack of Baltimore', available: http://www.baltimore.ie/heritage-history/the-sack-of-baltimore-1631.html [Accessed 12 August 2011].

BBC News (2005). 'Crucified nun dies in 'exorcism'', available: http://news.bbc.co.uk/go/pr/fr/-/2/hi/europe/4107524.stm [Accessed 23 February 2011].

BBC News (Africa) (2010). 'Burundi albino boy 'dismembered'', available: http://www.bbc.co.uk/news/world-africa-11614957 [Accessed 24 October 2010].

BBC News (UK) (2004). 'Garda quiz two over African death', 18 August, available: http://news.bbc.co.uk/2/hi/europe/3576038.stm [Accessed 30 August 2011].

BBC News (UK) (2005). 'Boys 'used for human sacrifice'', available: http://news.bbc.co.uk/2/hi/uk_news/4098172.stm [Accessed 24 August 2011].

BBC News (UK) (2010). 'Seedy underworld of human trafficking', available: http://news.bbc.co.uk/2/hi/uk_news/northern_ireland/8675275.stm [Accessed 7 June 2011].

BBC News (UK) (2011a). 'Prostitution ring boss Thomas Carroll faces £1.9m order', available: http://www.bbc.co.uk/news/uk-wales-12731409 [Accessed 7 June 2011].

BBC News (UK) (2011b). 'Trafficked children 'sold in UK for £16,000'', available: http://www.bbc.co.uk/news/uk-politics-13440736 [Accessed 29 July 2011].

Bhaumik, S. (2010). 'India 'human sacrifice' suspected in West Bengal temple', BBC News, available: http://news.bbc.co.uk/2/hi/8624269.stm [Accessed 24 August 2011].

Bourke, A. (1999). *The Burning of Bridget Cleary*, New York: Penguin.

Bowen, C. (2008). 'Minister welcomes fine for migrant worker exploitation', available: http://www.minister.immi.gov.au/media/media-releases/2008/ce08024.htm [Accessed 3 September 2011].

Brady, T. & Phelan, S. (2011). 'Kids in HSE care ended up working in brothels', *Irish Independent*, 3 June [Accessed 31 August 2011].

Brennan, S.M. (2009). 'The Writings: Excerpts from Masseen Sorcery', available: http://intothedarkness.tripod.com/id47.html [Accessed 5 November 2011].

Brison, S.J. (2002). *Aftermath: Violence and the Remaking of a Self*, Princeton, NJ: Princeton University Press.

Brison, S.J. (2006). 'Contentious freedom: Sex work and social construction', *Hypatia*, Vol. 21 No. 4, pp. 192-200.

Buckley, M. (2004). 'Evil trade', *The World Today*, Vol. 60, Issue 8/9, pp. 30-32.

Burkhalter, H. (2004). 'Health consequences of sex trafficking', available: http://www.childtrafficking.com/Docs/burkhalter_h_2004_health_cons equences_of_sex_trafficking_7.pdf [Accessed 18 August 2011].

Burnham, O. (2000). *African Wisdom*, London: Piatkus Books.

Carlow People (2010). 'Brothel boss gets seven years in jail', available: http://www.carlowpeople.ie/news/brothel-boss-gets-seven-years-in-jail-2054558.html [Accessed 7 June 2011].

Carrell, S. (2005). 'Campaign to pardon the last witch, jailed as a threat to Britain at war', *The Guardian*, 13 January 2007, available: httpp://www.guardian.co.uk/uk/2007/jan/13/secondworldwar.world [Accessed 5 August 2011].

Catholic Information Service for Africa (CISA) (2007). 'Witchcraft destroying the Catholic Church in Africa, experts say', *Catholic Online*, 2 September, available: http://www.catholic.org/international/ international_story.php?id=22994 [Accessed 8 March 2012].

Central Intelligence Agency (CIA) (2011). 'The World Factbook', available: https://www.cia.gov/library/publications/the-world-factbook/geos/ ni.html [Accessed 10 August 2011].

Chambers, V. (2007). 'The *Witchcraft Act* wasn't about women on brooms', *The Guardian*, 24 January, available: http://www.guardian.co.uk/ commentisfree/2007/jan/24/comment.comment3 [Accessed 10 March 2012].

Channel 4 (2010a). *The Hunt for Britain's Sex Traffickers: Series 1, Episode 2*, 1 September, 21h.

Channel 4 (2010b). *The Hunt for Britain's Sex Traffickers: Series 1, Episode 3*, 2 September, 21h.

Children's Rights Alliance (2010). 'Irish State at bottom of EU to stop sex trafficking of children while Irish public leads the way, raising €30,000 in funds', available: http://www.childrensrights.ie/ index.php?q=knowledgebase/child-protection/irish-state-bottom-eu-stop-sex-trafficking-children-while-irish-publi [Accessed 27 July 2011].

Christoph, H., Müller, K.E. & Müller, U.R. (2000). *Soul of Africa: Magical Rites and Traditions*, Cologne: Könemann Verlagsgesellschaft mbH.

Cimpric, A. (2010). 'Children accused of witchcraft: An anthropological study of contemporary practices in Africa', available:

http://www.unicef.org/wcaro/wcaro_children-accused-of-witchcraft-in-Africa.pdf [Accessed 13 September 2010].

Cole, J. (2006). 'Reducing the damage: Dilemmas of anti-trafficking efforts among Nigerian prostitutes in Palermo', *Anthropologica*, Vol. 48, No. 2, pp. 217-228.

Collins, N. & O'Shea, M. (2000). *Understanding Corruption in Irish Politics*, Cork: Cork University Press.

Comaroff, J. & Comaroff, J. (1999). 'Occult economies and the violence of abstraction: Notes from the South African postcolony', *American Ethnologist*, Vol. 26, No. 2, pp. 279-303.

Criminal Law (Human Trafficking) Act, 2008, No. 8 of 2008, Dublin: Government Publications.

Criminal Law (Sexual Offences) Act, 1993, No. 20 of 1993, Dublin: Government Publications.

Crowley, A. (1938). *The Book of the Law*, Berlin: Ordo Templi Orientus.

Csordas, T. (1994). *The Sacred Self: A Cultural Phenomenology of Charismatic Healing*, Berkeley: University of California Press.

Cusack, J. (2010a). 'African girls trafficked by evil, violent pimps', *Sunday Independent*, 7 February 2010.

Cusack, J. (2010b). 'It's business as usual for sex trade', *Irish Independent*, 25 July, available: http://www.independent.ie/opinion/analysis/its-business-as-usual-for-sex-trade-2271700.html [Accessed 18 February 2012].

Dan, P. (1649). *Histoire de Barbarie, et de ses corsaires. Des royavmes, et des villes d'Alger, de Tvnis, de Salé, & de Tripoly. Divisée en six livres. Ov il est traitté de levr govvernement, de leurs mœurs, de leurs cruautez, de leurs brigandages, de leurs sortileges, & de plusieurs autres particularitez remarquables. Ensemble des grandes miseres et des crvels tourmens qu'endurent les Chrestiens captifs parmy ces infideles*, Paris: Chez P. Rocolet.

David, F. (2008). 'Trafficking of women for sexual purposes', Australian Institute of Criminology (AIC), available: http://www.aic.gov.au/documents/1/C/E/%7B1CE51DE9-5346-4565-A86B-778F895BF9E1%7Drpp95.pdf [Accessed 21 June 2011].

Davies, C. (2010). 'Couple jailed after using trafficked girls in huge prostitution ring: Nigerians aged from 15 to 21 forced to work in business controlled from former vicarage in Wales', *The Guardian*,

available: http://www.guardian.co.uk/uk/2010/feb/04/wales-
prostitution-nigeria-court-carroll [Accessed 7 June 2011].

Dean, J. (2002). 'If anything is possible', in Knight, P. (ed.), *Conspiracy
Nation: The Politics of Paranoia in Postwar America*, New York: New York
University Press, pp. 85-106.

Department of Justice & Equality (2010). 'Ireland ratifies *UN Convention on
Transnational Organised Crime and Human Trafficking Protocol*', available:
http://www.justice.ie/en/JELR/Pages/Ireland%20ratifies%
20UN%20Convention%20on%20Transnational%20Organised%20Crim
e%20and%20Human%20Trafficking%20Protocol [Accessed 10 June
2011].

Department of Justice & Equality (2011). 'BlueBlindfold.gov.ie: Garda
operations', available: http://www.blueblindfold.gov.ie/website/bbf/
bbfweb.nsf/page/whatisbeingdone-gardaoperations-en [Accessed 10
June 2011].

Department of Justice, Equality & Law Reform (n.d.). *National Action Plan
to Prevent and Combat Trafficking of Human Beings in Ireland 2009-2012*,
Dublin: Department of Justice, Equality & Law Reform,.

Douglas, M. (2003). *The Lele of the Kasai* [1963], New York: Routledge.

Durkheim, E. (1947). *The Elementary Forms of Religious Life: A Study in
Religious Sociology*, New York: Free Press.

Ehrenreich, B. & English, D. (1973). *Witches, Midwives and Nurses: A History
of Women Healers*, New York: Feminist Press at CUNY.

Ejorh, T. (n.d.). 'Immigration and citizenship: African immigrants in
Ireland', available: http://www.ucd.ie/mcri/immigration_and_
citizenship.pdf [Accessed 12 October 2010].

Elabor-Idemudia, P. (2003). 'Migration, trafficking and the African
woman', *Agenda*, Vol. 58, pp. 101-116.

Ellis, S. and Ter Haar, G. (2004). *Worlds of Power: Religious Thought and
Political Practice in Africa*, London: C. Hurst & Co.

Escort Ireland (n.d.). 'Irish escorts: Sligo escorts', available:
http://www.escort-ireland.com/18/sligo-escorts.html [Accessed 29
August 2011].

European Institute for Crime Prevention and Control affiliated with the
United Nations (HEUNI) (2011). 'Trafficking for forced labour and
labour exploitation in Finland, Poland and Estonia', available:
http://www.heuni.fi/Satellite?blobtable=MungoBlobs&blobcol=urldata
&SSURIapptype=BlobServer&SSURIcontainer=Default&SSURIsession=

false&blobkey=id&blobheadervalue1=inline;%20filename=HEUNI%20r
eport%2068.pdf&SSURIsscontext=Satellite%20Server&blobwhere=1296
728524945&blobheadername1=Content-Disposition&ssbinary=
true&blobheader=application/pdf [Accessed 29 June 2011].

Evans-Pritchard, E.E. (1937). *Witchcraft, Oracles and Magic Among the Azande of the Anglo-Egyptian Sudan*, Oxford: Clarendon Press.

Evans-Pritchard, E.E. (1976). *Witchcraft, Oracles and Magic Among the Azande of the Anglo-Egyptian Sudan*, Oxford: Oxford Press.

Fanning, B., Killoran, B., Ní Bhroin, S. & McEvoy, G. (2011). 'Taking racism seriously: Migrants' experiences of violence, harassment and anti-social Behaviour in the Dublin Area', Immigrant Council of Ireland, available: http://www.immigrantcouncil.ie/images/
stories/191680_Immigrant_council_report_Final_with_cover.pdf
[Accessed 6 March 2012].

Feingold, D.A. (2005). 'Think again: Human trafficking', *Foreign Policy*, Vol. 150, No. 32, available: http://www.foreignpolicy.com/articles/2005
/08/30/think_again_human_trafficking?page=0,3 [Accessed 28 August 2011].

Fisher, H.J. (1979). 'Dreams and conversion in Black Africa', in Levtzion, N. (ed.), *Conversion to Islam*, New York: Holmes & Meier Publishers, Inc., pp. 217-35.

Foxcroft, G. (2009). 'Witchcraft accusations: A protection concern for UNHCR and the wider humanitarian community?', available: http://www.steppingstonesnigeria.org/images/pdf/witchcraft_accusatio
ns.pdf [Accessed 10 March 2012].

Frazer, J.G. (1996). *The Golden Bough: A Study in Magic and Religion*, New York: Touchstone Press.

Gammelli, C. (2011). 'Haiti children being sold for €1 in wake of quake chaos', *Irish Independent*, 21 February 2011.

Gardner, G. (2004a). *The Meaning of Witchcraft* [1959], Boston: RedWheel/
Weiser.

Gardner, G. (2004b). *Witchcraft Today* [1954], New York: Citadel Press.

George W. Bush Administration (2003). 'National Security Presidential Directive 22: Trafficking in persons', 25 February, available: http://www.fas.org/irp/offdocs/nspd/trafpers.html [Accessed 29 August 2011].

Geschiere, P. (1997). *The Modernity of Witchcraft: Politics and the Occult in Postcolonial Africa*, Charlottesville: University of Virginia Press.

Gibbons, J. (1998). 'Development in the study of the great European witch hunt', available: http://draeconin.com/database/witchhunt.htm [Accessed 8 August 2010].

Ginzburg, C. (1983). *The Night Battles: Witchcraft and Agrarian Cults in the Sixteenth and Seventeenth Centuries*, Baltimore: Johns Hopkins University Press.

GMANews.tv (2008). 'Aussie firm gets record fine of $174K for exploiting Pinoy, Irish workers', 3 December, available: http://www.gmanews.tv/ story/84469/pinoy-abroad/aussie-firm-gets-record-fine-of-174k-for-exploiting-pinoy-irish-workers [Accessed 6 September 2011].

Goode, E. & Ben-Yehuda, N. (1994). *Moral Panics: The Social Construction of Deviance*, Malden, MA: Blackwell Publishers.

Goodey, J. (2004). 'Sex trafficking in women from Central and East European countries: Promoting a "victim-centred" and "woman-centred" approach to criminal justice intervention', *Feminist Review*, Vol. 76 (*Post-Communism: Women's Lives in Transition*), pp. 26-45.

Goodstein, L. (2010). 'For Catholics, interest in exorcism is revived', *The New York Times*, 12 November, available: http://www.nytimes.com/ 2010/11/13/us/13exorcism.html [Accessed 16 February 2012].

Harris, P. (2002). 'Thames torso boy was sacrificed', *The Guardian*, 2 June, available: http://www.guardian.co.uk/uk/2002/jun/02/ ukcrime.paulharris [Accessed 26 October 2010].

Hayes, S. (1995). 'Christian responses to witchcraft and sorcery', *Missionalia*, Vol. 23, No. 3, pp. 339-354.

Haynes, D.F. (2004). 'Used, abused, arrested and deported: Extending immigration benefits to protect the victims of trafficking and to secure the prosecution of traffickers', *Human Rights Quarterly*, Vol. 26, No. 2, pp. 221-272.

Health Service Executive (2009). *Health Services Intercultural Guide: Responding to the Needs of Diverse Religious Communities and Cultures in Healthcare Settings*, Dublin: Health Service Executive.

Immigration Residence and Protection Bill, 2010, No. 38 of 2010, Dublin: Government Publications.

Integrated Regional Information Networks (IRIN) (2005). 'Pakistan: Focus on kidney sales by bonded labourers', available: http://www.irinnews.org/report.aspx?reportid=28499.

International Labour Organization (ILO) (1930). *Convention concerning Forced or Compulsory Labour*, available: http://www.ilo.org/ilolex/cgi-lex/convde.pl?C029 [Accessed 9 August 2011].

International Labour Organization (ILO) (2005). 'Human trafficking and forced labour exploitation - guidance for legislation and law enforcement, available: http://www.ilo.org/wcmsp5/groups/public/---ed_norm/---declaration/documents/publication/wcms_081999.pdf [Accessed 9 August 2011].

International Labour Organization (ILO) (2005). *A Global Alliance against Forced Labour: Global Report under the Follow-up to the* ILO Declaration on Fundamental Principles and Rights at Work, 2005, Geneva: International Labour Organisation.

International Organization for Migration (IOM) (n.d.). 'The nature of human trafficking, available: http://www.iom.int/jahia/Jahia/about-migration/managing-migration/pid/676 [Accessed 22 December 2010].

Irish Aid (2011). 'Overview', available: http://www.irishaid.gov.ie/about.asp [Accessed 6 August 2011].

Irish Examiner (2011). 'Human trafficking: Lack of Irish convictions masks deadly truth of trafficking', available: http://www.examiner.ie/ireland/human-trafficking-lack-of-irish-convictions-masks-deadly-truth-of-trafficking-141070.html [Accessed 7 June 2011].

Irish Examiner (2011). 'Human trafficking: Lack of Irish convictions masks deadly truth of trafficking', *Irish Examiner*, 4 January 2011.

Jenkins, P. (2000). *Mystics and Messiahs: Cults and New Religions in American History*, New York: Oxford University Press.

Jimmyjay (2009). 'Irish escort reviews: Review 018296', available: http://www.escort-ireland.com/18296/Joanne/review.html.

John, C. (2005). 'Exorcisms are part of our culture', BBC News Online, 3 June, available: http://news.bbc.co.uk/2/hi/uk_news/4596127.stm [Accessed 3 November 2011].

Joon, K.K. & Fu, M. (2008). 'International women in South Korea's sex industry: A new commodity frontier', *Asian Survey*, Vol. 48, No. 3, pp. 492-513.

JRank Science and Philosophy (2011). 'Witchcraft– the social and political history of witchcraft in Europe, the functions of witchcraft, symbolic and ideological aspects of witchcraft', available: http://science.jrank.org/pages/8157/Witchcraft.html [Accessed 6 August 2011].

Kaim, T. (2008). 'Black and white witchcraft: A cultural crossroads in Paris inspires therapeutic innovation', available: http://www.psychotherapy.net/article/black-white-witchcraft [Accessed 26 October 2010].

Kapferer, B. (ed.) (2003). *Beyond Rationalism: Rethinking Magic, Witchcraft and Sorcery*, New York: Berghahn Books.

Kapstein, E.B. (2006). 'The New Global Slave Trade', *Foreign Affairs*, Vol. 85, No. 6, pp. 103-115.

Kara, S. (2009). *Sex Trafficking: Inside the Business of Modern Slavery*, Columbia University Press [Online], [Accessed 30 August 2011].

Kara, S. (2011). 'Eyewitness account: Child labor in North India's hand-woven carpet sector', *GoodWeave*, Spring 2011.

Kelleher, P., O'Connor, M. & Pillinger, J. (2009). *Globalisation, Sex Trafficking and Prostitution: The Experiences of Migrant Women in Ireland*, Immigrant Council of Ireland [Online], available: http://www.immigrantcouncil.ie/images/stories/Trafficking_Report_FULL_LENGTH_FINAL.pdf [Accessed 15 June 2011].

Kim, K. & Hreshchyshyn, K. (2005). 'Human trafficking private right of action: Civil rights for trafficked persons in the United States', *Hastings Women's Law Journal*, Vol. 16 (2004 -2005), pp. 1-36.

King, S. (2011). 'Crusade against trafficking may be missing the point on sex industry', *Irish Examiner*, 6 July 2011.

Korps landelijke politiediensten (2008). 'Schone schijn: de signalering van mensenhandel in de vergunde prostitutiesector [Keeping Up Appearances: The Signs of Human Trafficking in the Legalized Prostitution Sector]', 1 July, available: http://www.om.nl/publish/pages/98059/klpd_sneep_low_res_tcm5-968601.pdf.

Korvinus, A., van Dijk, E., de Jonge van Ellemeet, H., Koster, D. & Smit, M. (2005). *Trafficking in Human Beings: Fourth Report of the Dutch National Rapporteur*, available: http://english.bnrm.nl/Images/Rapportage%204%20(Eng)_tcm64-83608.pdf [Accessed 25 January 2012].

Lally, C. (2010a). 'Life inside an Irish brothel: Prostitution in Ireland: Part Two', *The Irish Times*, 10 May 2010, p. 1.

Lally, C. (2010b). 'A pimp's family business', *The Irish Times*, available: http://www.2010againstpoverty.eu/export/sites/default/downloads/Journalist_Award/JA_IR.pdf [Accessed 7 June 2011].

Lally, C. (2010c). 'Police officer overheard Carroll directing punters to brothels', *The Irish Times*, p. 4.

Lane-Poole, S. & Kelley, J.D.J. (1970). *The Barbary Corsairs*, Westport, CT: Negro Universities Press.

Lanning, K. (1992). 'Investigator's Guide to Allegations of 'Ritual' Child Abuse', Quantico, VA: FBI Behavioural Science Unit, Mind Control and Ritual Abuse Information Service website, available: http://sites. google.com/site/mcrais/fbisra [Accessed 8 August 2010].

Lee, M. (2007). *Human Trafficking*, Cullompton, Devon: Willan.

London Metropolitan Police Service (2010). 'Man sentenced for trafficking and rape', available: http://content.met.police.uk/News/Man-sentenced-for-trafficking-and-rape/1260267460932/1257246745756 [Accessed 18 August 2011].

Makori, H. (2008). 'Opinion: Why Christianity fails to be a 24/7 religion in Africa', *Catholic Information Service for Africa* (CISA), 103 (7 October).

Mbiti, J. (n.d.). 'General manifestions of African religiosity: An exploratory paper at the first meeting of the standing committee on the contributions of Africans to the religious heritage of the world', available: http://www.afrikaworld.net/afrel/mbiti.htm [Accessed 3 November 2010].

McDougall, D. (2006). 'Indian cult kills children for goddess', *The Observer*, 5 March 2006, available: http://www.guardian.co.uk/world/2006/mar/05/india.theobserver [Accessed 24 August 2011].

Migrant Rights Centre Ireland (2006). 'No way forward, no going back: Identifying the problem of trafficking for forced labour in Ireland', available: http://www.mrci.ie/media/File/No%20Way%20 Forward%20-%20No%20Going%20Back%20-%20Trafficking%20for %20forced%20labour%20in%20Ireland.pdf [Accessed 26 July 2011].

Miller, J.R. (2008). 'Call it slavery', *The Wilson Quarterly* (1976-), Vol. 32, No. 3, pp. 52-56.

Moody, G. & Moody, E. (n.d.). *African, Nigerian and Santeria Witchcraft*, End-Time Deliverance Ministry, available: http://www.demonbuster.com/ african5.html [Accessed 16 February 2012].

Murray, M. (1921). *The Witch-Cult in Western Europe: A Study in Anthropology*, Oxford: Clarendon Press.

Murray, T.D. (2006). 'Baltimore to Barbary: The 1631 sack of Baltimore', *History Ireland*, Vol. 14, No. 4, pp. 14-18.

Nam, J.S. (2007). 'The case of the missing case: Examining the civil right of action for human trafficking victims', *Columbia Law Review*, Vol. 107, No. 7, pp. 1655-1703.

National Rapporteur on Trafficking in Human Beings (2010). *Human Trafficking: Ten Years of Independent Monitoring*, available: http://english.bnrm.nl/Images/8e%20rapportage%20NRM-ENG-web_tcm64-310472.pdf [Accessed 18 June 2011].

NGO Alliance Against Racism (2011). *Shadow Report: In Response to the Third and Fourth Periodic Reports of Ireland under the UN International Convention on the Elimination of All Forms of Racial Discrimination*, available: http://www.immigrantcouncil.ie/images/stories/NAAR_Shadow_Report_to_CERD_final.pdf [Accessed 6 March 2012].

Nic Gabhan, S. (2006). 'Human trafficking: A twenty-first century slavery', *The Furrow*, Vol. 57, No. 10, pp. 528-537.

Norfolk, A. (2011). 'Some of these men have children the same age; they are bad apples', *The Times*, 5 January 2011.

Nwolisa, E.C.P.O. (n.d.). 'Social and cultural changes in Nigerian society: The role of household in women/young girls trafficking as ebony/exotic1 bodies in the European sex industry', available: http://soc.kuleuven.be/ceso/dagvandesociologie/papers/Exotic%20bodies%20in%20the%20European%20market%20economy.pdf [Accessed 6 March 2012].

O'Brien, C. (2009). 'Three men jailed for trafficking into Ireland', *The Irish Times*, 3 December 2009.

O'Brien, L. (2005). *Irish Witchcraft from an Irish Witch*, Franklin Lakes, NJ: Career Press.

O'Clery, C. (2010). 'African sex slaves forced to work in Irish brothels', *GlobalPost*, available: http://www.globalpost.com/dispatch/ireland/100521/African-women-sex-slaves-human-trafficking [Accessed 7 June 2011].

O'Doherty, C. (2010). 'Witchcraft and threats used against trafficked workers', *Irish Examiner*, 25 May, available: http://www.examiner.ie/ireland/witchcraft-and-threats-used-against-trafficked-workers-120708.html. [Accessed 26 October 2010].

Ofuoku, M. (1999). 'Sex export: Dirty details of young Nigerian girls being sent to Europe for prostitution', *Newswatch: Nigeria's Weekly Magazine*, 31 July.

Olaniyi, R. (2003). 'No way out: The trafficking of women in Nigeria', *Agenda*, No. 55, pp. 45-52.

Organization for Security and Co-operation in Europe (OSCE) (2008). 'Human trafficking for labour exploitation/forced and bonded labour:

Identification – prevention – prosecution', available:
http://www.ungift.org/doc/knowledgehub/resource-
centre/OSCE_Human_Trafficking_for_Labour_Exploitation.pdf
[Accessed 29 July 2011].

Organization for Security and Co-operation in Europe (OSCE) (n.d.).
'Factsheet on preventing and combating trafficking in human beings in
the OSCE region', available: http://www.osce.org/cthb/74755 [Accessed
29 July 2011].

Parish, J. (2010). 'Circumventing uncertainty in the moral economy: West
African shrines in Europe, witchcraft and secret gambling', *African
Diaspora*, No. 3, pp. 77-93.

Phillips, R. (2011), 'The haunting story of how Adam, the Torso in the
Thames boy, was finally identified', *MailOnline*, available:
http://www.dailymail.co.uk/news/article-1375024/Voodoo-human-
sacrifice-The-haunting-story-Adam-Torso-Thames-boy-finally-
identified.html [Accessed 24 August 2011].

Pócs, É. (1998). *Between the Living and the Dead: A Perspective on Witches and
Seers in the Early Modern Age*, Budapest: Central European University
Press.

Polisen (2010). *Situation Report 11: Människohandel för Sexuella och Andra
Ändamål [Trafficking in Human Beings for Sexual and Other Purposes]*,
Swedish National Police Board [Online], available: http://www.si.se/
upload/Human%20Trafficking/L%C3%A4g%2011%20Fin%20ENG.PDF
[Accessed 29 July 2011].

Pontificial Council for Justice and Peace (2004). *Compendium of the Social
Doctrine of the Church*, available: http://www.vatican.va/roman_curia/
pontifical_councils/justpeace/documents/rc_pc_justpeace_doc_2006052
6_compendio-dott-soc_en.html [Accessed 8 March 2012].

Pope Benedict XVI (2005). 'Migrations: A sign of the times', Message of His
Holiness Benedict XVI for the 92nd World Day of Migrants and
Refugees (2006), available: http://www.vatican.va/holy_father/
benedict_xvi/messages/migration/documents/hf_ben-
xvi_mes_20051018_world-migrants-day_en.html [Accessed 8 March
2012].

Pope Paul VI (1965). *Gaudium et Spes: Pastoral Constitution on the Church in
the Modern World*, available: http://www.vatican.va/archive/
hist_councils/ii_vatican_council/documents/vat-
ii_cons_19651207_gaudium-et-spes_en.html [Accessed 8 March 2012].

Poudel, P. & Carryer, J. (2000). 'Girl-trafficking, HIV / AIDS and the position of women in Nepal', *Gender and Development*, Vol. 8, No. 2, pp. 74-79.

Pringle, Y. (2010). 'Fear, witchcraft and 'superstition' in East Africa', *Colonial Psychiatry Hub*, 21 March, available: http://www.colonialpsychiatry.net/2010/03/21/fear-witchcraft-and-%E2%80%98superstition%E2%80%99-in-east-africa/#_ftn6 [Accessed 6 August 2011].

Reilly, J. (2010). 'The happy hooker myth is a far cry from reality', available: http://www.independent.ie/national-news/the-happy-hooker-myth-is-a-far-cry-from-reality-2083480.html [Accessed 7 June 2011].

Remensnyder, S., Kregg, C. & Berg, S.M. (2005). 'Captive Daughters: Conference on Pornography and International Sex Trafficking', *Off Our Backs*, Vol. 35, No. 7/8, pp. 17-37.

Rogers, C. (2011a). 'Where child sacrifice is a business', BBC News, 11 October, available: http://www.bbc.co.uk/news/world-africa-15255357 [Accessed 12 October 2011].

Rogers, S. (2011b). 'Human trafficking: A life of vice is never voluntary', *Irish Examiner*, 4 January 2011.

RTÉ News (Ireland) (2004). 'Man released in Onyemaechi death probe', 18 August, available: http://www.rte.ie/news/2004/0818/onyemaechip.html [Accessed 30 August 2011].

RTÉ News (Ireland) (2011a). 'Ireland's last witch trial investigated', available: http://www.rte.ie/news/2011/0330/witches.html [Accessed 30 March 2011].

RTÉ News (Ireland) (2011b). 'Jailed brothel keeper ordered to pay €2m', available: http://www.rte.ie/news/2011/0314/carrolltj.html [Accessed 7 June 2011].

RTÉ Press Centre (2012). 'Prime Time -"Profiting From Prostitution"', available: http://www.rte.ie/about/pressreleases/2012/0204/040212primetime.html [Accessed 17 February 2012].

Ruhama (2011). *2010 Statistics Report*, available: http://www.ruhama.ie/easyedit/files/2010statsreportruhama.pdf [Accessed 25 August 2011].

Ruhama (n.d.). 'About Ruhama' [Online], available: http://www.ruhama.ie/page.php?intPageID=4 [Accessed June 7 2011].

Schepers, I. (2011). 'Operation Sneep: "The frayed edges of licensed prostitution"', in the *Alliance against Trafficking in Persons Expert Seminar on Leveraging Anti-Money Laundering Regimes to Combat Human Trafficking*, Vienna, 4 October, 3 pp.

Seymour, St. John (1913). Irish Witchcraft and Demonology, Baltimore, MD: Norman, Remington, available: http://www.forgottenbooks.org/ info/ 9781440053436 [Accessed 9 November 2010].

Shatter, A. (2011). 'Written answers - Proposed legislation', in *Dáil Éireann Debate*, Vol. 731, No. 5, Dáil Éireann, 2011: House of the Oireachtas.

Siegel, D. (2009). 'Human trafficking and legalized prostitution in the Netherlands', *Temida*, Vol. 12, No. 1, available: http://www.vds.org.rs/File/Tem0901.pdf [Accessed 15 June 2011].

silo (2009). 'Girls who won't haggle', available: http://www.escort-ireland.com/boards/showthread.php?t=19143 [Accessed 31 August 2011].

Simmons, D. (2000). 'African witchcraft at the millennium: Musings on a modern phenomenon in Zimbabwe', *Journal of the International Institute*, Vol. 7, No. 2.

Smyth, J. (2010). 'Hidden abuse of diplomats' domestics', *The Irish Times*, 27 November, B4.

Smyth, J. (2011). 'Eleven minors pursuing asylum go missing', *The Irish Times*, 10 January, available: http://www.irishtimes.com/newspaper/ ireland/2011/0110/1224287156483.html [Accessed 14 Dec 2011].

Stone, A. & Vandenberg, M. (1999). 'How the sex trade becomes a slave trade: The trafficking of women to Israel', *Middle East Report*, No. 211, pp. 36-38.

Summers, M. (ed. & tr.) (1971). *Malleus Maleficarum of Kramer and Sprenger*, Mineola, NY: Dover Publications.

Sunday World (2010). 'Voodoo sex traffickers', available: http://www.sundayworld.com/columnists/sw-irish-crime.php? aid=4050 [Accessed 7 June 2011].

Taussig, M. (1980). *The Devil and Commodity Fetishism in South America*, Chapel Hill, NC: University of North Carolina Press.

Taussig, M. (1997). *The Magic of the State*, New York: Routledge.

The Times (2011). 'Organised gangs, vulnerable girls: a pattern of exploitation unfolds', *The Times*, 5 January 2011.

The Times of India (2009). 'Girl's body found, black magic suspected', *The Times of India*, 2 November, available: http://timesofindia.indiatimes.com//city/surat/Girls-body-found-black-magic-suspected/articleshow/5190449.cms [Accessed 24 August 2011].

The Victims of Trafficking and Violence Protection Act, Public Law 106-386, 114
   Stat. 1464, Washington, DC: United States Government Printing Office.
Theodoropoulos, N. (2000). *Shamanism* [Online], available:
   http://www.paganspath.com/meta/uva/shaman.htm [Accessed 6
   August 2011].
Thylefors, M. (2009). "Our Government is in Bwa Kayiman': A Vodou
   ceremony in 1791 and its contemporary significations', *Stockholm
   Review of Latin American Studies*, No. 4, March, available:
   http://www.lai.su.se/gallery/bilagor/SRoLAS_No4_6.%20%E2%80%9D
   Our%20Government%20is%20in.pdf [Accessed 8 August 2011].
Tlhagale, B. (n.d.). *Bringing the African Culture Into the Church* [Online],
   available: http://www.afrikaworld.net/afrel/tlhagale.htm [Accessed 21
   February 2011].
Townsend, M. (2011). 'Sex trafficking in the UK: One woman's horrific
   story of kidnap, rape, beatings and prostitution', *The Observer*, 6
   February 2011, available: http://www.guardian.co.uk/uk/2011/feb/
   06/sex-traffick-romania-britain [Accessed 18 August 2011].
Turn Off The Red Light (n.d.). 'What is Turn Off The Red Light', available:
   http://www.turnofftheredlight.ie/ [Accessed 7 September 2011].
Ugba, A. (2004). 'A quantitative profile analysis of African immigrants in
   21st century Dublin', unpublished thesis (MPhil in Ethnic and Racial
   Studies), Trinity College Dublin.
Ugba, A. (2009). *Shades of Belonging: African Pentecostals in 21st Century
   Ireland*, Trenton, NJ: Africa World Press.
UNAIDS (2009). 'Fact sheet: Sub-Saharan Africa', available:
   http://www.unaids.org/en/media/unaids/contentassets/dataimport/pub
   /report/2009/20091124_FS_SSA_en.pdf [Accessed 16 February 2012].
UNESCO (2006). *Human Trafficking in Nigeria: Root Causes and
   Recommendations* [Online], available: http://unesdoc.unesco.org/
   images/0014/001478/147844e.pdf [Accessed 7 June 2011].
United Nations (1957). *Convention on the Abolition of Slavery, the Slave Trade,
   and Institutions and Practices Similar to Slavery, Supplementary to the
   International Convention Signed at Geneva on September 25, 1926*, Geneva,
   September 7, 1956, London: H.M. Stationery Office.
United Nations (2001). 'The race dimensions of trafficking in persons -
   especially women and children', in *World Conference against Racism,
   Racial Discrimination, Xenophobia and Related Intolerance*, Durban, South
   Africa, March 2001: United Nations Department of Public Information.

United Nations Children's Fund (UNICEF) Innocenti Research Centre (2004). *Trafficking in Human Beings, especially Women and Children, in Africa*, available: http://www.unicef-irc.org/publications/pdf/trafficking-gb2ed-2005.pdf [Accessed 15 June 2011].

United Nations Committee on the Elimination of Discrimination Against Women (2010). 'Responses to the list of issues and questions with regard to the consideration of the combined fourth to seventh periodic report: Uganda', CEDAW/C/UGA/Q/7/Add.1, 21 September, available: http://daccess-dds-ny.un.org/doc/UNDOC/GEN/G10/450/15/PDF/G1045015.pdf?OpenElement [Accessed 24 August 2011].

United Nations Office on Drugs and Crime (2000). *United Nations Convention against Transnational Organized Crime and its Protocols* [Online], available: http://www.unodc.org/unodc/en/treaties/CTOC/index.html#Fulltext [Accessed 10 June 2011].

United Nations Office on Drugs and Crime (2004). *United Nations Convention against Transnational Organized Crime and the protocols thereto*, New York: United Nations.

United Nations Office on Drugs and Crime (n.d.). *Human Trafficking* [Online], available: http://www.unodc.org/unodc/en/human-trafficking/what-is-human-trafficking.html#What_is_Human_Trafficking [Accessed 17 December 2010].

United States Department of Health & Human Services (n.d.). 'Sex trafficking: Fact sheet', available: http://www.acf.hhs.gov/trafficking/about/fact_sex.pdf [Accessed 18 August 2011].

United States Department of State (2005). *Trafficking in Persons Report 2005*, Washington, DC.

United States Department of State (2008). *Trafficking in Persons Report 2008*, Washington, DC.

United States Department of State (2009). *Trafficking in Persons Report 2009*, Washington, DC.

United States Department of State (2010). *Trafficking in Persons Report 2010*, Washington, DC.

United States Department of State (2011). *Trafficking in Persons Report 2011*, Washington, DC.

Upadhyaya, K.P. & Anti-Slavery International (2008). *Poverty, Discrimination and Slavery: The Reality of Bonded Labour in India, Nepal and Pakistan*, London: Anti-Slavery International.

Vaughan, M. (1983). 'Idioms of madness: Zomba lunatic asylum, Nyasaland, in the colonial period', *Journal of Southern African Studies*, Vol. 9, No. 2, pp. 218-38.

Vera, D. (2005). 'Is Satanism 'Pagan'?', Theistic Satanism, available: http://theisticsatanism.com/pagan/Is-Satanism-Pagan.html [Accessed 5 August 2011].

Viuhko, M. & Jokinen, A. (2009). *Trafficking for Sexual Exploitation and Organised Procuring in Finland, 62*, Helsinki: European Institute for Crime Prevention and Control, affiliated with the United Nations (HEUNI).

Vogel, E. (2011). 'Hearing witness says Nevada is haven for sex traffickers', *Las Vegas Review-Journal*, No. 6 (April), available: http://www.lvrj.com/news/hearing-witness-says-nevada-is-haven-for-sex-traffickers-119368459.html [Accessed 29 August 2011].

Walsh, M. (n.d.). 'Trafficking in Human Beings – Ireland's response', available: http://www.blueblindfold.gov.ie/website/bbf/bbfweb.nsf/da0ca5e9740185518025735500606068dd/757f3f8956f36359802575d8004f8e17/$FILE/Childlinks%20Article.pdf [Accessed 1 September 2011].

Wilson, P.L. (2003). *Pirate Utopias: Moorish Corsairs & European Renegadoes*, Brooklyn, NY: Autonomedia.

World Synod of Catholic Bishops (1971). 'Justitia in Mundo (Justice in the World)', in *Ministerial Priesthood and Justice in the World*, Vatican City, Rome, 1971: Vatican.

Xinhuanet.com (2006). '3 Indonesian tribesmen get death for ritual killings', 14 February, available: http://news.xinhuanet.com/english/2006-02/14/content_4178452.htm [Accessed 24 August 2011].